Farmers
Against the Crown

Farmers Against the Crown

A Comprehensive Account
Of the Revolutionary War Battle
In Ridgefield, Connecticut,
April 27, 1777

SECOND EDITION

By
Keith Marshall Jones III

Connecticut Colonel Publishing Company
Ridgefield, Connecticut
2003

Cover Illustration:

Detail from:
"A Skirmish in America between the Kings Troops and Genl. Arnold."
Etching, artist unknown, London, dated 14 April 1780.

Courtesy of the Keeler Tavern Preservation Society, Inc.

Please direct all correspondence and book orders to:
Connecticut Colonel Publishing Company
304 Farmingville Road
Ridgefield, Connecticut 06877

Library of Congress Control Number 2002101579
ISBN 0-9709703-1-5

Published for Connecticut Colonel Publishing Company
by Gateway Press, Inc., 1001 N. Calvert Street
Baltimore, MD 21202-3897

Printed in the United States of America

Contents

Acknowledgments

The Americans who fought at Ridgefield would never have emerged from their obscure twenty-first-century hiding places if not for assistance from the staffs at the following institutions: Connecticut Historical Society, Danbury Public Library, Fairfield Public Library, Fairfield Historical Society, Greenwich Public Library, Hiram Halle Library of Pound Ridge, Keeler Tavern Preservation Society, Lewisboro Public Library, Mark Twain Library of Redding, North Salem Public Library, Norwalk Public Library, Pequot Library of Southport, Ridgefield Public Library, Stamford Public Library, Sterling Memorial Library at Yale University, Stratford Public Library, Westchester County Historical Society, Wilton Public Library, and Woodbury Public Library,

I am particularly grateful to Connecticut State Historian Christopher Collier for innumerable nuances only a professional eye could add. Special thanks to Damon Douglas, author of the monograph *The Bridge not Taken* (an important re-assessment of Benedict Arnold's role at Saugatuck Bridge published under the auspices of the Westport Historical Society), for constructively challenging my manuscript at a critical point.

If biographers should be hardy enough to fill the page of history with the advantages that have been gained with unequal numbers (on the part of the Americans) in the course of this contest, and attempt to relate the distressing circumstances under which they have been obtained, it is more than probable that posterity will bestow on their labors the epithet and marks of fiction; for it will not be believed that such a force as Great Britain has employed for eight years in this country could be baffled, in their plan of subjugating it, by numbers infinitely less, composed of men oftentimes half starved, always in rags, without pay, and experiencing, at times, every species of distress which human nature is capable of undergoing.

George Washington to Nathaniel Greene February 6, 1783

I. Prologue

Resplendent in a spotless, shocking scarlet full-dress uniform glittering with heavy gold epaulets, and topped off with long-plumed hat, British Lieutenant General John Burgoyne surrendered his sword along with what remained of his 7,800-man army to General Horatio Gates on October 17, 1777, thereby sealing the surprising Patriot victory at Saratoga. With a respectful nod of the head, Gates immediately returned Burgoyne's sword and invited his former adversary (and pre-war fellow King's officer) into his marquee for refreshments. During the ensuing meal shared by senior staff of both armies, Burgoyne praised (to Gates' discomfort) the battlefield performance of one particular American officer — General Benedict Arnold — whose bravery and skill at Freeman's Farm and Breymann's Redoubt had twice carried the day for Rebel arms.

Arnold, however, lay in agony on an Albany hospital bed, his left leg shattered from battlefield heroics. Saratoga was a turning point, if not *the* turning point of the American Revolution, and Arnold as George Washington's "fighting general" had ample reason for self-satisfaction despite his painful slow-healing wound. Benedict Arnold had every right to savor Saratoga's glory, for less than six months earlier this ambitious, financially obsessed, self-consumed, yet thoroughly able officer was unhorsed by redcoat musket fire and forced to abandon the field in an engagement given little more than passing mention by most historians.

Early that Sunday afternoon of 27 April 1777, Arnold had led a hastily assembled collection of Fairfield County militia and patriotic farm boys, augmented by a handful of equally raw Continental troops, against British regulars more than three times their number at the sleepy, out-of-the-way, southwestern Connecticut village of Ridgefield. Sandwiched between George Washington's startling Trenton/Princeton successes and subsequent British victories at Brandywine and Germantown, the affair was but a small sideshow in the American Revolution's grand eight-year drama. What's more, the engagement itself was a freak of timing that, if Benedict Arnold is to be believed, would never have happened had British troops under General William Tryon reached Ridgefield two hours earlier.[1]

Tryon, however, did not expect to be engaged at all. Having previously decoyed Continental Army units westward to the Hudson River, the British command hoped to take out George Washington's supply depot in Danbury without resistance. Besides, southwestern Connecticut contained large numbers of Loyalists, and a show of strength just might return the countryside to King George III. But Tryon and his superior, Sir William Howe, did not anticipate area farmers and local militia companies would turn out in force to face a professional army. And, albeit slowly, turn out they did! In response to the Danbury alarm, militia companies from as far as New Haven, Litchfield, Woodbury, and New Milford were set in motion. From all ten Fairfield County chartered towns — even from Westchester County, New York — farmers and shopkeepers hoisted muskets and headed for regimental rendezvous points, then on to Ridgefield.

Newspaper accounts of the subsequent action contrasted sharply depending upon editorial predisposition. Pro-American papers, such as New Haven's *Connecticut Journal* of April 30, 1777, described the Ridgefield fray as a full-fledged battle "which continued about an hour, in which our men behaved with great spirit, but being overpowered by numbers, were obliged to give way."

Seething with anger still palpable to modern readers two-and-a-quarter centuries later, the *Boston Gazette* of May 5th vented its rage at Tryon, "whose blood thirsty thievish disposition and beggarly circumstances impel him to plunder for subsistence, having collected a gang of thieves and starved wretches..." Loyalist journals, on the other hand, lauded General Tryon's successful Danbury raid and, like the May 5th

New York Gazette, dismissed Ridgefield as a brief skirmish "carried after small opposition, with considerable loss on the side of the rebels."

The Revolution (or Rebellion, depending upon one's perspective) ran its remarkable course until the Treaty of Paris was signed in 1783, by which time the Ridgefield engagement was all but forgotten. To be sure, historians on both sides of the Atlantic soon touched dutifully on Tryon's expedition and its Ridgefield footnote in a wave of voluminous, often ponderous, retrospectives; however, these accounts offered little real detail about the action itself, focusing instead on General David Wooster's gallant demise and Benedict Arnold's heroics.[2] Mid-nineteenth-century American authors, such as Barber, Hollister, and Lossing, revisited the Ridgefield affair, but charged with nationalism these less than objective accounts leaned heavily on romantic episodes such the cannonball still wedged in corner post of Ridgefield's historic Keeler Tavern.[3]

Danbury historian James Case's short 1927 piece was the first to explore matters in real depth. Prepared on the raid's 150th anniversary, *An Account of Tryon's Raid on Danbury* devoted five full pages to the Ridgefield fray. That same anniversary year, local historian George Lounsbury Rockwell also had much to say about the engagement in his classic *History of Ridgefield.* Although Rockwell provided valuable insight on Revolutionary War contributions of individual soldiers, his lack of source documentation and heavy reliance on oral tradition produced a wandering, folksy, altogether one-sided account of the battle itself. Almost half a century later, on the eve of America's 1976 bicentennial celebration, Robert F. McDevitt's *Connecticut Attacked: A British Viewpoint of Tryon's Raid on Danbury* set the record straight with a dispassionate, scrupulously researched essay based on original sources, particularly the eyewitness diary of British Captain Archibald Robertson. While McDevitt is unlikely to be surpassed in scholarship, a mere nine pages, alas, were devoted to the Ridgefield theatre of the British raid.

Smithsonian Institution curator, prolific author, and longtime Ridgefield resident, Silvio Bedini comes closest to the mark with his 1958 *Ridgefield in Review,* followed by an essay in the Spring 1987 *Connecticut Historical Society Bulletin* entitled "A Skirmish in America: A Rare Etching and the Battle of Ridgefield." The first work provides more than twenty pages of pertinent background information concerning the battle/skirmish, while the latter meticulously documents the origin and history of a circa-1780 London print still gracing historic Keeler Tavern Museum. Regrettably, neither account reconstructs the action in fullest detail.

One hungers for more. Who were the farmers that left plows in the field and families at the hearth, and often lacking ammunition, responded with their neighbors to the Danbury alarm? What actually happened when these amateur soldiers collided with the cream of British arms in the streets of Ridgefield? How were the American troops deployed and what transpired after their defensive barricade was breached? What kind of men were these redcoats, anyway, and how did they behave when securing the town?

In search of answers, I have endeavored here to provide the most comprehensive coverage of the Ridgefield action yet assembled. The formal reports of senior officers from both sides (Arnold, Silliman, Tryon and Sir William Howe), together with British Captain Archibald Robertson's eyewitness diary, provide a sound foundation for the narrative — but only a foundation. To discover what really happened that bloody April day, students of history must climb down from generals' horses and mingle with the rank and file. After all, 2,500 soldiers and hundreds of ordinary townsfolk also witnessed the action. Only by piecing together dozens of lesser figure eyewitness recollections, relevant government documents, multiple town-biographical histories, family papers and traditions, does the full story emerge.

This approach is not without risk, for family tradition wisely warns Connecticut State Historian Christopher Collier, "is the lowest rung on the ladder of evidential credibility."[4] But history is more than just a collection of generally accepted dates and places; it's also the spontaneous product of human sweat and individual quirks. Most participants in the Ridgefield fray were too busy dodging musket balls and bayonets to write things down, but that doesn't mean their stories must be ignored. Besides, we can be sure that for every piece of oral tradition that *has* survived, dozens of equally arresting actual incidents have gone unrecorded. Nonetheless, these captivating vignettes should not be confused with proven facts. To distinguish word-of-mouth spice from certified meat in the historical stew pot, I have employed three different typeface approaches in this piece. Eyewitness passages and corroborated second person accounts are shown in **boldface**; credible secondary source material appears in regular type, while pure oral tradition has been *italicized*. All are documented by endnote in the final section of this work.

Almost as tricky are labels of national affiliation. Exactly what do we call those who rallied against British arms at Ridgefield? Continental Congress, after all, rendered "colonist" obsolete by declaring the "United States of America" independent only nine months before. "American" is just plain confusing since Revolutionaries and loyal Crown subjects alike considered themselves American; furthermore both camps prized state citizenship above any newfound federal status. Therefore I have simply described the combatants in their own language: those siding with Congress dubbed themselves "Patriots" while the King's man considered himself "Loyalist." When period tempers flared, opponents were more colorfully dubbed "Rebel" or "Tory," a practice to which this piece also resorts as temperatures rise.

Hopefully then, readers will experience the events of April 27, 1777 as a terribly *human* story, rather than simply a heavily footnoted series of facts strung together by a time-line. "All well and good," one might reply, "but isn't there anything really *new* here?" To which the answer is a grateful "yes!" When various accounts from the past two-and-a-quarter centuries were assimilated, it became clear that the Patriot defense of Ridgefield continued for some time after the formal barricade "Battle" had concluded. Drawing upon veteran pension records, participant diaries, family genealogies and, yes, local histories and tradition, this work is the first to focus in some detail on what happened after the barricade was breached and Benedict Arnold had withdrawn to Saugatuck. In particular, I have tried to identify the fate of individual soldiers and also clarify the organized resistance on the "Rising Ground above the Village" referred to in Captain Robertson's eyewitness diary. Perhaps most satisfying of all, the names of several Patriots buried anonymously near the Ridgefield barricade can be revealed for the first time.

Making its first appearance ever is a detailed, house-by-house, street-by-street map of Ridgefield center in April 1777. Product of more than a hundred hours research through Town Hall land transaction records, this never-before-seen glimpse of the village provides a birds-eye view of the running battle that swept down its mile-long central thoroughfare. Because a surprising number of pre-Revolutionary structures remain standing in one form or another (and to appease those who insist in keeping at least one foot in the present century), this work closes with a present-day photo tour of General Tryon's trail through the twenty-three square mile township.

Still, the question remains: "Was the day's work in Ridgefield really a full-scale battle... or merely a skirmish?" That is for you, the reader, to decide for yourself! For now, try to imagine a traveler retiring to an upstairs bedchamber of Timothy Keeler Junior's smoke-filled eighteenth-century tavern in this out-of-the way Connecticut farm town. A few hours earlier, an agitated horseman had vaulted from his foam-drenched mount and burst into the tavern taproom. "The redcoats are looting and burning Danbury," he might have said, "and Ben Stebbins' boy, Josiah, has turned Tory and gone over to them." What would tomorrow bring?

II. Southwestern Connecticut in 1777

Tavern owner Timothy Keeler Jr. would have failed to see the humor in common British reference to 1777 as the "year of the hangman"— a double entendre connecting the sequence of gibbet-like sevens with the anticipated fate of George Washington and his rebel cronies. As the War for Independence entered a third year, the Patriot commander-in-chief was comfortably ensconced in winter headquarters at Jacob Arnold's tavern on the common in Morristown, New Jersey pondering the upcoming spring campaign. Washington guessed that Crown forces would either attempt to separate New England from the middle colonies by commandeering the North River (Hudson) from New York through Lakes George and Champlain to Montreal, or try to take Philadelphia — or both. To counter the King's potential initiatives, Continental regiments were subsequently deployed like so many chess pieces in four locations: Lake Champlain; the Delaware River between Philadelphia and the Atlantic; the Jersey plains; the Hudson Highlands.[1]

Champlain, anchoring the northern flank of Washington's defensive axis, was defended from Canada-based assault by a "Northern Army" led by General Philip Schuyler who posted a strong force at Fort Ticonderoga under General Anthony Wayne. Delaware River forts Mifflin and Mercer were garrisoned to protect Philadelphia from a sudden water-borne thrust out of British-occupied New York. Creating flexibility to quickly unite his army for a rapid dash in either direction, Washington concentrated the main body of his troops at two key stations: Middlebrook, New Jersey (Generals Nathaniel Greene and Israel Putnam) and Peekskill, New York (General Alexander McDougall). Both Middlebrook and Peekskill were also well placed to interrupt livestock and fodder sale to redcoat quartermasters by less than patriotic New York and New Jersey farmers as winter gave way to spring.

In reality though, Washington's main army had virtually dissolved by March 1777! Because most Continental enlistments expired in December '76, the Commander-in-Chief's entire New Jersey force was fewer than three thousand, two thirds of which was militia. Artfully masking his desperate situation by repeatedly countermarching the remnants along the front in a false display of strength while mercilessly harassing small British foraging parties, General Washington pleaded with individual state governors for reinforcements. Desperation transcending formality, his letter of March 5th to Governor Jonathan Trumbull, urged immediate dispatch of 2000 Connecticut militia to Peekskill:

> **I am persuaded, from the readiness with which you have ever complied with all my demands, that you will exert yourself in forwarding the aforementioned number of men, upon my bare request. But I hope you will be convinced of the necessity of the demand, when I tell you, in confidence, that after the 15th of this month... I shall be left with the remains of five Virginia regiments, not amounting to more than as many hundred men, and parts of two or three other continental battalions, all very weak. The remainder of the army will be composed of small parties of militia from this state and Pennsylvania, on whom little dependence can be put, as they come and go when they please.[2]**

Governor Trumbull's response took the form of ten militia regiments (two from Fairfield County) totaling 2000 men under General Jeremiah Wadsworth, who were ordered to Peekskill by the State Council of Safety on March 20th. Citing ill health, Wadsworth declined the honor, and a week later Trumbull named General Erastus Wolcott to go in his stead. The two Fairfield County levies (13th and 16th militia regiments) didn't actually march until August,[3] but by early April relief units from the newly organized (January 1777) Connecticut Continental Line began funneling into Peekskill. Although Howe was yet to tip his strategic hand, His Excellency suspected Sir William would move on Philadelphia, and began shifting the Peekskill troops into New Jersey.

Despite General Washington's fears, little had changed on the ground north of New York since the indecisive Battle of White Plains in October 1776, following which American forces hardened along a permanent defensive line protecting Peekskill and Connecticut's southwestern frontier. Barely fifteen miles southwest of Ridgefield, this thin cordon extended eastward from the Hudson (then known as North River), along the Croton River, across Northern Westchester County and a small portion of Connecticut (known as "Horseneck") to Long Island Sound. Another fifteen miles farther south, just above heavily fortified Kings Bridge, the roughly parallel perimeter of British-controlled New York stretched across Yonkers and Eastchester. In between lay a bloody no-man's-land known as the *neutral ground.* This buffer zone of prosperous Dutch manor-grant farmland had been worked for a century by tenants, grantees, and offspring of the baronial Van Cortland, Phillipse and DeLancey families, but was rapidly degenerating into a "dog's breakfast" of partisans, refugees, spies, and scoundrels of every sort.

Here marauding bands of Loyalist irregulars such as James DeLancey's light horse raided local farms to supply redcoat quartermasters with replacement mounts and regimental mess tables with meat. Dubbed "cowboys" for their livestock-rustling prowess, DeLancey and his ilk terrorized Westchester County, kidnapping prosperous farmers, ambushing rebel militia companies, and engaging Continental cavalry patrols. Less honorable cowboy gangs were capable of much worse. Little wonder, then, Patriot farmers such as Major Samuel Lyons[4] of Bedford abandoned homesteads located by misfortune in the neutral ground and sought protection in Connecticut.

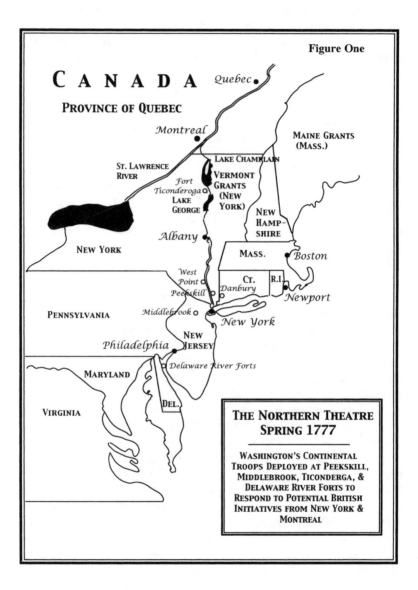

Figure One

CANADA   Quebec

PROVINCE OF QUEBEC

Montreal

MAINE GRANTS
(MASS.)

ST. LAWRENCE
RIVER

LAKE CHAMPLAIN

Fort
Ticonderoga
LAKE
GEORGE

VERMONT
GRANTS
(NEW
YORK)

NEW
HAMP-
SHIRE

Albany

NEW YORK

MASS.

Boston

West
Point
Peekskill

CT.   R.I.

Danbury

Newport

PENNSYLVANIA

Middlebrook

New York

Philadelphia

NEW
JERSEY

Delaware River Forts

MARYLAND

DEL.

VIRGINIA

**THE NORTHERN THEATRE
SPRING 1777**

WASHINGTON'S CONTINENTAL
TROOPS DEPLOYED AT PEEKSKILL,
MIDDLEBROOK, TICONDERGA, &
DELAWARE RIVER FORTS TO
RESPOND TO POTENTIAL BRITISH
INITIATIVES FROM NEW YORK &
MONTREAL

Loyalist neutral-ground farmers fared no better. Seized for sale at "blackrate" (a confiscation practice employed by Whig and Tory alike) their property often passed to Rebel refugees whose own homesteads behind British lines had been similarly usurped by opportunistic Tories. As one sympathetic King's officer penned in a September 1776 diary:

> **The Rebels are committing great outrages on the loyalists in West Chester County, and are selling their effects by public auction. Many of the loyal inhabitants of this Province whom the Rebels carried away lately into New England, have been removed again from the places of their confinement, to others of which their friends are ignorant.[5]**

Adding to the confusion, squadrons of Continental Army light horse, led by knowledgeable Westchester County partisan guides such as Abraham Dyckman and Cornelius Oakley, engaged in nighttime saber encounters as they returned from reconnoitering behind British lines. But most dangerous of all were ragged collections of freebooters and Whig outlaws called "skinners," (perhaps after the notorious Cortlandt Skinner) who operated as free-lance highwaymen, "skinning" all comers of possessions in nighttime raids. One junior Continental officer, William Hull, who would later earn a brigadier general's star, recalled that: **"skinners would leave victims hung by their arms, or even their thumbs, on barn doors, dangling in agony from wounds inflicted in defense of their property."[6]** In truth, few asked whether a stolen rooster crowed for Congress or King, and a handsome farm steed was considered fair game for cowboys, skinners, partisans and soldiers alike.

To the east, refugee migrations between Connecticut and British-held Long Island precipitated similar conditions with Long Island Sound as an aquatic neutral zone. Displaced dependents such as the widow Betty McCloskey and her five children fled Long Island for the safety of inland Ridgefield, while Connecticut Loyalists escaped eastward under cover of darkness. Nutmeg state merchants and farmers openly exchanged wares with their Long Island Loyalist counterparts (a practice glibly called "London trading") in return for British-manufactured necessities such as window glass, tools, and paper. Less scrupulous traders dealt directly with British quartermasters who tendered the King's gold for cattle, horses and fodder.

By nightfall all pretense of commercial truce along the Sound vanished as parties of nautical "skinners" plundered contraband traders, and Loyalist whaleboat sorties from Long Island raided the Connecticut seacoast, robbing homes of absent soldiers and kidnapping prominent Patriots. Even Fairfield County militia commander Gold Selleck Silliman was roused from bed in his Fairfield home on the dark night of May 2, 1779, spirited-away by whaleboat across the sound, and held nearly a year before being ransomed.[7] With equal flair, local sons of liberty returned such favors, while Patriot militia units known as Coast Guards patrolled Fairfield County's shoreline waters.

To Connecticut's west, Hudson River forts Montgomery, Clinton, and Constitution were garrisoned to protect the highlands from a long anticipated British up-river thrust toward Albany. A massive iron-link chain and accompanying wooden boom stretched across the Hudson above Peekskill, while the town itself was transformed into a staging area for newly formed Continental Line regiments. Danbury, only ten miles northeast of Ridgefield, had become the Continental Army's primary northern supply depot, where livestock, gunpowder, barreled beef and flour, tents and uniforms were assembled for drovers to relay to General Washington's Middlebrook and Peekskill encampments.

Studded with small family farms, inland Connecticut's southwestern corner was knit together by a hilly network of narrow dirt roads, really no more than upgraded Indian trails or primitive cart-paths that enabled local farmers to bring crops to market and families to church. Perched in the middle of this agricultural oasis were three of Fairfield County's ten chartered towns — Danbury, Ridgefield and Redding. With a combined population of 5,468 in 1774, this threesome contained fewer souls than Stratford, then Fairfield County's most populous town.[8] To be certain, the surrounding settlements of Wilton, Norfield (Weston), and New Canaan all existed, but only as parishes of Norwalk, Fairfield, and Stamford, just as Bethel and Ridgebury were respective parishes of Danbury and Ridgefield.

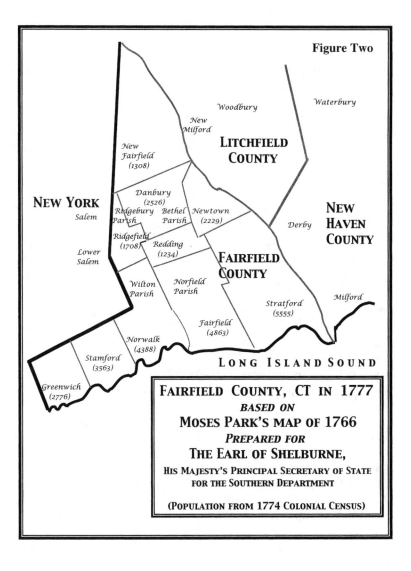

Figure Two

FAIRFIELD COUNTY, CT IN 1777
BASED ON
MOSES PARK'S MAP OF 1766
PREPARED FOR
THE EARL OF SHELBURNE,
HIS MAJESTY'S PRINCIPAL SECRETARY OF STATE
FOR THE SOUTHERN DEPARTMENT

(POPULATION FROM 1774 COLONIAL CENSUS)

Except for its remarkable mile-long, eight-rod-broad (132 feet) main street, sleepy self-sufficient Ridgefield was a typical rural Yankee hamlet. Twenty-eight homestead plots, distributed by lottery to the original proprietors in 1712, fronted this broad thoroughfare, then known as "Town Street." Each plot consisted of a two-and-one-half-acre residential lot plus a five-acre planting field to the rear. The planting acres, in turn, were bounded to the back by access roads that paralleled Town Street to form an elongated north-south grid. After 1725 the surrounding land to the east and west had also been divided by lottery, denuded of forest, and transformed into prime plow-land. Since most Town Street homesteads sported barns, outbuildings and a small fruit orchard, the cultivated little ridge-top settlement possessed a bucolic air — and copious quantities of apple cider.

No drawing, engraving or map survives to show us how the village appeared that April in the year of the hangman, but the location of every dwelling lay hidden in land record logs lodged in the bowels of Town Hall. After poring over hundreds of eighteenth-century land transactions, the author was able to construct a house-by-house schematic of Ridgefield as it might have looked 225 years ago. (See *Figure Three* on page 16.) Because most of the community's 1,708 souls inhabited 200-or-so unpretentious farmhouses scattered throughout six outlying school districts, the village itself was sparsely inhabited by today's standards, containing perhaps sixty dwellings clinging to Town Street.

Most village houses were simple post-and-beam-framed one-and-a-half or two-story saltboxes, whose modest twenty-by-thirty-foot dimensions surrounded a huge center chimney. More prosperous residents, such as Benjamin Hoyt, Colonel Philip Burr Bradley, and the descendants of Reverend Thomas Hauley enjoyed more spacious gambrel-roofed accommodations with two full floors, gable-windowed attics and multiple chimneys. Book-ended by local tanner Benjamin Stebbins' circa-1718 residence at its north end, and Timothy Keeler's Tavern to the south, the broad ridge-crest Town Street connected Ridgefield by passenger and post with the outside world.

Overnight Keeler Tavern lodgers who cared to engage townsfolk on a mid-day stroll would have soon discovered that

Ridgefield funded its own schools, maintained its own dirt roads, hired its own ministers and, lacking river power to drive heavy mills, engaged in little commerce beyond its borders. And three generations after the town's founding, most families in town were connected by marriage! Local interdependency was further cemented by religion, for three out of four churchgoers worshipped beneath a single roof — the First Ecclesiastical Society, better known as the Congregational Church. Prominently situated on a huge common, smack in the middle of Town Street, the facility also served as both town meeting house and schoolroom. Specifically mandated by the state legislature to receive financial support, the Congregational Society enjoyed a significant advantage over its only rival, St. Stephen's Anglican Church located about a quarter-mile to the north.

Children were pre-Revolutionary Ridgefield's most abundant crop, for the 1774 Provincial Census revealed more than 34% of town population to be less than ten years of age... and almost 60% were under twenty. Given the brutal realities of eighteenth-century rural life, it is not surprising the same census recorded only eleven males and thirteen women beyond the age of 70 — a mere 1.4% of the total population![9] Supporting these two cohorts were the yeoman landholders, known as "freemen," and their industrious and very likely pregnant wives.

Because Ridgefield's 250-or-so local freemen were roughly economic equals, society was mercifully spared polarization that often accompanied disparate living standards. Still, hard specie was scarce, and in a statewide absence of banks, the local economy was fueled by barter. Blacksmith, miller, nail-maker, limekiln operator, tanner, doctor, and farmer alike were thus linked to their neighbors by a complex network of mutual accounts. Most citizens were of English descent and all were subjects of the British Crown, so there were no really divisive political issues before the Revolution. Except for governor, lieutenant governor, and state senator (then known as governor's assistant), all elective offices were local, and each chartered Connecticut town dispatched two representatives (deputies) to the state legislature, which beginning in 1774 selected participants to attend the Continental Congress. None were from Ridgefield.

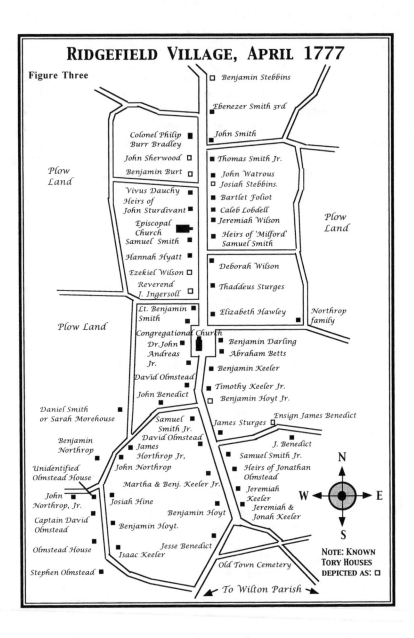

Ridgefield Village, April 1777

Figure Three

Benjamin Stebbins

Ebenezer Smith 3rd

John Smith

Colonel Philip Burr Bradley

John Sherwood

Benjamin Burt

Plow Land

Thomas Smith Jr.

John Watrous

Josiah Stebbins.

Vivus Dauchy Heirs of John Sturdivant

Bartlet Foliot

Caleb Lobdell

Jeremiah Wilson

Episcopal Church Samuel Smith

Heirs of 'Milford' Samuel Smith

Plow Land

Hannah Hyatt

Ezekiel Wilson

Deborah Wilson

Reverend J. Ingersoll

Thaddeus Sturges

Lt. Benjamin Smith

Elizabeth Hawley

Northrop family

Plow Land

Congregational Church

Dr. John Andreas Jr.

Benjamin Darling

Abraham Betts

David Olmstead

Benjamin Keeler

John Benedict

Timothy Keeler Jr.

Benjamin Hoyt Jr.

Daniel Smith or Sarah Morehouse

Samuel Smith Jr.

James Sturges

Ensign James Benedict

Benjamin Northrop

David Olmstead

James Horthrop Jr,

John Northrop

J. Benedict

Samuel Smith Jr.

Unidentified Olmstead House

Martha & Benj. Keeler Jr.

Heirs of Jonathan Olmstead

John Northrop, Jr.

Josiah Hine

Benjamin Hoyt

Jeremiah Keeler

Jeremiah & Jonah Keeler

Captain David Olmstead

Benjamin Hoyt.

Olmstead House

Jesse Benedict

Isaac Keeler

Old Town Cemetery

Stephen Olmstead

N
W · E
S

Note: Known Tory Houses depicted as: ◻

To Wilton Parish

The Journey from King to Congress

Revolution was the farthest thing from Connecticut's collective mind when church bells clanged across the Colonies in January 1763 celebrating cessation of the bloody French and Indian Wars. Redcoats and colonials had fought together from Virginia to Quebec for seven years, during which no colony provided military support more faithfully than Connecticut. In fact, the wartime journal of British Commander-in-Chief Sir Jeffrey Amherst noted Connecticut exceeded all other colonies in troop subscriptions by delivering 86.9% and 100% of his requests respectively in 1761 and 1762.[10]

Although repulsed by slave-like treatment of the redcoat rank and file, and disgusted by arrogant British officers under which they served, returning Yankee volunteers took pride in their heightened status as Englishmen. And for good reason! All of North America east of the Mississippi, from Canada to Florida, was under undisputed British control, while the Indian menace had been driven from New England once and for all. What's more, Crown forces had also wrested the West Indies islands of St. Vincent, Dominica, Tobago, Grenada, and the Grenadines from French hands — temporarily ending generations of molasses smuggling that fueled New England's burgeoning rum distilling business. As citizens of the world's most powerful empire (India, Minorca, Senegal, and the Philippines were further prizes of war), and beneficiaries of a global trading network secured by the unchallenged Royal Navy, most colonists saw themselves not just as Englishmen, but full-fledged partners with the mother country.

Of course, reasonable men on both sides of the Atlantic believed that America should assume some fair share of the £146,000,000 debt racked up by Great Britain at war's end, as well as an equitable portion of the ongoing cost to maintain a string of Royal garrisons still guarding the western frontier. The question was how to do so without sacrificing the colonists' perceived natural rights and violating the constitutional protection of Englishmen to be taxed only with their consent.   And here, reasonable men began to disagree.

In most Colonies, particularly Massachusetts, Virginia and New York, the "no taxation without representation" position was vociferously served up by duly elected legislatures to crown-appointed colonial governors. Inevitably, frustration arose as these worthies turned a deaf ear to such arguments and legislative blood began to boil. *But not in Connecticut!* Unlike its sister colonies, Connecticut (along with Rhode Island) had been granted a direct charter from the King in 1662, under which its governor was selected by the freeholders — not by the British government. Since each chartered town dispatched two locally elected representatives to the Assembly, Connecticut's government was in fact a creature of the people, not of the King. And so in 1764, Governor Thomas Fitch and the Connecticut General Assembly agreed to represent their interests in Parliament by sending an agent to lobby influential ministers of the King's government. Selected for the task was prominent New Haven lawyer and judge Jared Ingersoll — brother of longtime Ridgefield Congregational Church minister Jonathan Ingersoll.

While Jared Ingersoll, along with Pennsylvania agent Benjamin Franklin watched, listened, and presumably lobbied whoever might lend an ear, Parliament passed two of the most controversial laws ever to affect the Colonies: the Quartering Act and the Stamp Act of 1765. Ingersoll had no reason to quarrel with the former, with its provision that barracks be erected at local expense for redcoat regiments, because there were simply no British troops stationed in Connecticut then or later. His discrete silence as the Stamp Act steamrollered through Parliament was rationalized in a long letter to Governor Fitch:

> **The point of authority of Parliament to impose such tax I found was so fully and universally yielded that there was not the least hopes of making any impression that way.** [11]

Perhaps mistaking Jared Ingersoll's discretion for compliance, Prime Minister Sir George Grenville then asked him to recommend the distributor for his Majesty's stamps in Connecticut. Ingersoll gave the matter (and the position's 7.5% commission) careful consideration... and nominated himself!

The ill-conceived Stamp Act was immediately nullified in America by violence. Stamps bound for Connecticut were seized from the brig commanded by a Captain Haviland in New York harbor and destroyed by local Sons of Liberty.[12] Mobs took to the streets of Boston, New York, and Newport, terrifying the newly appointed stamp distributors to resign. Word of this northern response spread quickly and all other colonial distributors also stepped down. There were no successors. As for Ingersoll, he was accosted by several hundred Sons of Liberty in Wethersfield en route to a special session of the Connecticut General Assembly and judiciously tendered a roadside resignation:

> ... which he read himself in the hearing of the whole company. He was then desired to pronounce the words Liberty and Property, three times, which having done the whole body gave three cheers. Mr. Ingersoll then went to a tavern and dined with several of the company.[13]

Nine months later, an embarrassed Parliament repealed the ill-fated Stamp Act.

It is unlikely that out-of-the way Ridgefield was much concerned by these affairs; period town meeting records are blank on the subject. While intellectually interesting, parliamentary maneuvers 3,700 miles away were just not relevant to simple western Connecticut farmers. In Ridgefield there were no redcoats to quarter, no printers or lawyers dependent upon stamped papers and, unlike coastal trading towns such as New Haven or Fairfield, no seagoing merchants whose trade may have suffered nor mob of unemployed or otherwise disgruntled laborers with time and liquor on their hands. As to the proposed stamp tariff on playing cards, country farmers had little time for such distractions anyway. Besides, the governor was a Connecticut man, not some London clubroom crony. While the pot continued to boil in Boston and Williamsburg,

Ridgefielders remained good British subjects, absorbed the Loyalist counsel of Reverend Ingersoll, and went about their business.

Suddenly, in the fall of 1774, external events burst in upon this tranquil, self-sufficient little enclave. In response to the Boston "Tea Party," British Parliament closed the port of Boston and slapped colonists with four punitive statutes collectively known as the "Intolerable Acts." In turn the Virginia House of Burgesses called for the convening of a Continental Congress, which first came to order on September 5th, 1774 in Philadelphia's Carpenters Hall. Five weeks later this First Continental Congress issued a shocking resolution requesting each colony to switch allegiance from King George to the Congress itself by boycotting all things British!

Throughout Connecticut, property-owning freemen of each chartered town gathered to debate casting their collective fate with Congress or holding steadfast with Crown and Parliament. Moderated by Nathan Olmstead, and influenced no doubt by Congregational minister Ingersoll, Ridgefield freemen voted in town meeting 30 January 1775 to *reject* the Congressional request, and reaffirmed **"his Most Sacred Majesty King George the 3rd to be our rightful Sovereign."**[14] Only nine Patriots cast dissenting votes! In an astonishing display of self-satisfaction, the local assembly then agreed to transmit written copies of their decision to New York printers **"that they may be published to the world."**

In February 1775, a month after the freemen of both Ridgefield and Newtown chose King over Congress, Fairfield County's pro-Congress towns, led by Fairfield itself, voted to curtail trade with the two Loyalist communities. Because of its agricultural self-sufficiency and minimal merchant infrastructure, or perhaps because most residents simply preferred a course of quiet neutrality, Ridgefield shrugged off the boycott threat and continued to go about its business. But the matter would not go away; that April the question of allegiance resurfaced at a town meeting. Led by 84-year-old Loyalist Benjamin Stebbins as moderator, the freemen **"resolved not to open the Resolves of January."** Ranked fifth wealthiest of 253 entries on the Town Grand Tax List, Stebbins surely imagined that at his age more was to be lost than gained from independence. But now the Loyalist majority was weakening, and fifty-five exasperated Ridgefield freemen soon signed a statement disassociating from the town meeting decision.

Then came news that blood had been spilled at Lexington and Concord. Volunteer contingents were rushed to defend Boston by forty-seven of Connecticut's seventy chartered towns — but Ridgefield was not among them! While the town fathers dithered, local Patriots could wait no longer, particularly in Ridgebury Parish. Aroused by Congregational minister Samuel Camp, the freemen of Ridgebury (then known as the "Second Ecclesiastical Society") began holding meetings of their own and erected a liberty pole along the road to Ridgefield. Ridgebury Patriots Ichabod Doolittle and Gamaliel Northrop went so far as to enlist for a six-month tour of duty as junior officers in Fairfield County contingents bound for Boston. At least fourteen other townsmen followed.

Responding to the concerns of Governor Trumbull and the General Assembly, a 150-man party of Patriots set out from Fairfield in September 1775 to disarm and intimidate residents of Danbury, Redding and Ridgefield who refused to disavow the Crown, but local records are blank on the consequences. By November, returning veterans from the Boston siege helped form "committees of safety" throughout the state to replace local officials with proven Patriots. Bolstered by the return of Doolittle and Northrop, and encouraged by the passage of anti-Tory legislation in the General Assembly, a twenty-six-man Ridgefield "Committee of Inspection" was established in December. In addition to monitoring the comings and goings of suspected Loyalists, the committee immediately published a list of "enemies of the Liberties of America" with whom fellow townsmen were urged to have no further dealings. Benjamin Stebbins' shoemaker/tanner son Josiah, a French and Indian War veteran, was one of the first to be baptized an enemy by the list. Brought to trial for his Tory activities, Josiah posted a £300 bond, promised "quiet behavior" and returned home.

Patriot pressure to disavow King George extended well beyond compiling lists of enemies. The Loyalist-dominated Ridgefield Episcopal Church (Church of England) was forced to discontinue services altogether in July 1775, and minister Epenetus Townsend later complained of **"excessive vigilance of the rebel committees in getting and examining all letters."**[15] Refusing to take an oath of allegiance, Townsend was subsequently ordered on March 31, 1777 to depart within eight days.   Released from incarceration by Westchester County Patriots, Townsend apparently became chaplain to a New York British regiment, then perished at sea with his wife and five children when the unit was in transit to Nova Scotia.

Like his Episcopal counterpart, Congregationalist Reverend Jonathan Ingersoll also refused to break with Britain; but his services were not interrupted because, unlike Episcopal practice, Congregational litany did not incorporate allegiance to the monarchy. From one of New Hampshire's most respected families, Jonathan Ingersoll had occupied the local pulpit since 1739 and even accompanied Ridgefield men into the field during the French and Indian conflicts, serving in David Wooster's 4th Regiment in the Lake Champlain campaign of 1758. Clearly Ingersoll was a man to be reckoned with, an opinion leader to whom less-certain men paid attention.

Reverend Ingersoll and his New Haven lawyer brother notwithstanding, Ridgefield inched precariously into the Patriot fold by year-end. Town Street resident and Committee of Inspection leader, newly commissioned militia colonel Philip Burr Bradley replaced Benjamin Stebbins as town meeting moderator and under Bradley's leadership on December 17, 1775 the freemen resolved to **"adopt and approve of the Continental Congress for securing and defending the Rights and Liberties of ye United American Colonies."**[16] Eight months after Lexington, Ridgefield, at last, ceased to be on record as a "Tory" town!

A subsequent town meeting resolution went on to authorize armed support of the cause, offering £6 yearly to all who would enlist for up to three years. Sixty-four men immediately formed company with Gamaliel Northrop of Ridgebury as Captain, and James Betts and John St. John as Lieutenants. Later a second company formed under Captain David Olmstead. Northrop's company was assigned to the 4th Connecticut Militia (in General Wadsworth's Brigade) commanded by Colonel Gold Selleck Silliman, scion of a prominent Fairfield family. The Ridgefield men saw considerable action, beginning with the Brooklyn front and the Battle of Long Island in August 1776. Barely eluding capture on the retreat from New York in September, Northrop's company next fought at Harlem Heights and the Battle of White Plains, where young Corporal William Lee was killed.

As 1776 closed, the Cause was at low ebb. British General Henry Clinton had seized Newport Rhode Island and with naval support might ravage Connecticut. A continuous string of losses in the field had gutted morale and raised serious questions about George Washington's generalship. Why, for example, had His Excellency divided his outnumbered army between Long Island and New York when Howe's fleet hove to at Staten Island, and why were several regiments of Connecticut men left to be captured at Fort Washington on the lower Hudson?

Discouraged by shortages of food, clothing and equipment, their pay in arrears, whole companies melted away as annual enlistments expired. **"The existing army, except a few regiments affording an effective force of about fifteen hundred men, would dissolve in a few days,"**[17] remembered eyewitness John Marshall, future Chief Justice of the Supreme Court, then with Washington as lieutenant in the 11th Virginia Regiment. The remaining Continentals huddled together in winter camps, scattered widely by General Washington so a multiplicity of bonfires might disguise his emaciated numbers from the enemy.

The diary of one regimental quartermaster, Elisha Frisbie of Litchfield, refers to such encampments around Ridgefield, and to repeated stays at the Keeler Tavern by a stream of friends and relatives succoring sick soldiers encamped nearby. Filthy soldiers in crowded, unkempt camps spread both smallpox and dysentery throughout the colonies, and the Fairfield County encampments were no exception. In a letter to his father-in-law, the Reverend Joseph Fish, Colonel Silliman noted that dysentery in particular **"prevailed greatly and proved very mortal in some of our neighboring towns."**[18] Ridgefield vital records reveal twelve such deaths between September and December 1776, with five in the Platt family alone.

Wary Tories and Reluctant Patriots

Earlier in that discouraging year of 1776, future President John Adams poured out his frustrations in a letter from Philadelphia to his beloved Abigail. Characterizing the Continental Congress with his usual candor, Adams remarked: **"We were about one third Tories, and one third timid, and one third true blue."**[19]

Ridgefield, too, had its share of the timid and the Tory, despite the town decision to abandon King for Congress and ongoing oversight from the committee of inspection. Leading figures such as miller Daniel Sherwood, hatter Epenetus How(e), blacksmith Benjamin Burt, and merchant Benjamin Hoyt who inhabited the large gambrel-roofed house just south of Keeler Tavern, all remained loyal Crown subjects. But there was a price to be paid for such loyalty: according to Fairfield County records, at least thirty-three Ridgefielders, including Benjamin Hoit (Hoyt) were hauled into court for subversive behavior. George Folliot began as a Loyalist, but when dispatched to a Hartford jail in 1777 for his beliefs posted bond and took an oath of allegiance to the American cause. New Jersey's Tory governor, William Franklin, was not so fortunate. Despite the notoriety of being Benjamin Franklin's illegitimate son, William was confined "without pen and ink" in a Connecticut prison and disappeared from history until his 1803 death in England.

At this point in the hostilities, Loyalists could make a persuasive case. American armies had been continuously embarrassed in the field, and the ragged desertion-riddled remnants were starving in disease-ridden winter camps. Holders of Continental notes and currency suffered severe asset depreciation, while English pounds were coveted everywhere. And despite Jefferson's elegant Declaration of Independence, no European country, not even Britain's archrival France, had yet recognized the fledgling American government.

For these reasons and more, Sir William Howe, commander of His Majesty's North American ground forces, was experiencing great success in New Jersey with his "Free and General Pardon" that promised no retribution for rebels who returned to the British fold. And more than a few heads were turned by Tory boasts that the Rebels *"... had 13 kings and no bread, and that it was better to serve one king and have plenty of bread."*[20] In fact, two important American leaders — Richard Stockton of New Jersey and Joseph Galloway of Pennsylvania — publicly recanted and urged compatriots to follow their lead. Furthermore, the New Jersey legislature had disbanded in face of Howe's victorious army, and Continental Congress had fled from Philadelphia to safer quarters in Baltimore.

Energized by the proximity of British-controlled New York, prominent Connecticut Loyalists, such as the Reverend Richard Mansfield of Derby, whispered to undecided neighbors that a 20,000-man British army was headed their way, and that only those who immediately declared for the Crown could be sure of their estates. Such conjecture was no idle gossip, for strategists on both sides could plainly see that by capturing Philadelphia Howe might bring the rebellion to a close next spring. Not surprisingly, then, about half a million Americans throughout the Colonies, or roughly 20% of the total Caucasian population, remained loyal to King George III.[21] The number was probably much higher in Fairfield County, where prominent merchant Isaac Stiles' 1776 diary conservatively placed one of four in the Tory fold.

Although Fairfield County's so-called Tory towns (Redding, Ridgefield and Newtown) had produced Patriot majorities by 1777, Connecticut militia major general David Wooster warned as late as April **"... there may be greater danger from the western Tories than the [British] Regulars."**[22] It was with good reason, then, that His Majesty's generals assumed southwestern Connecticut might return to the crown if adroitly handled.

While local Patriot committees of safety intercepted mail, monitored comings and goings, searched private homes for tea and British goods (telltales of a Tory within), compiled enemies' lists and boycotted nonconformists, the Loyalist minority learned to communicate with one another in secret.

For some the next step was to volunteer information to His Majesty's forces, while others accepted payment for their services becoming in effect British spies.   After sweeping American forces off Long Island and investing York (Manhattan) Island, Sir William Howe wasted little time establishing a broad intelligence network around his new headquarters.   Paid to pass along news of troop movements and rebel supply depots, Connecticut agents such as Derby innkeeper Zechariah Hawkins, Moses Dunbar of Hartford, and Robert Thomson of Newtown plied their secret trade until ultimately uncovered by local committees of safety. Thomson, ironically, was convicted in Danbury on April 21, only five days before Tryon's redcoat army would arrive, and sent home to Newtown for execution.[23]

Redding was fertile ground for British sympathizers. The spy Andrew Patchen was captured twice, yet somehow avoided the noose, while Ephraim DeForest helped guide Tryon's troops and likely fought alongside the British at Ridgefield.   But for pure duplicity, William Heron takes the Redding cake. Member of the Connecticut General Assembly, town selectman, and trusted confidant of General Samuel H. Parsons (commander of the state Continental Line), Heron hedged his bets on the Revolution by spying for both sides! Under Crown pay as "Hiram, the spy," Heron personally delivered confidential information to the British Commander-in-Chief on frequent visits to New York under flag of truce ostensibly for mercantile purposes. The double agent then regurgitated his observations on Royal activity back to Parsons.[24]   Even General Parsons may have been keeping open a back door to the British camp, for both Sir Henry Clinton's private papers and his adjutant's diary noted an on-going private dialogue with Parsons:

> "A Correspondence has been for sometime past kept up with a Major General in the Rebel service, who commands part of the Connecticut troops. He has lately intimated their desire of joining us on certain terms, and declaring against Congress."[25]

Whatever his motives for corresponding with the enemy, Parsons always served the Rebel cause honorably, and like Heron, emerged from the War as a respected Patriot. Because "Hiram's" role as a paid British spy from 1776-1781 was not revealed until 1882, Heron continued to enjoy the respect of his Redding neighbors; but had the struggle ended differently his future under the Union Jack would likely have been equally secure.

While Heron hedged his bets in secret, the Reverend John Beach of Redding's Church of England spared no effort illuminating himself as an unwavering beacon of Anglicanism. Charismatic and truly devout, Reverend Beach stubbornly persisted with Anglican services in Redding, Newtown and Ridgefield, despite written warnings from local selectmen to desist. **"I preach frequently and administer the sacrament at Ridgefield..."** Reverend Beach wrote, **"... where there are about fourteen or eighteen families of very serious and religious people who have a just esteem of the Church of England, and are very desirous to have the opportunity of worshipping God in that way."**[26]

Reverend Beach's curious experience illustrates the complexity of Fairfield County Patriot/Loyalist relations during the early years of Revolution. Since 1737, Beach had administered baptisms, communions, marriages, and funerals, while dispensing spiritual advice from the Anglican pulpit. This forty-year stint of conscientious pastoral service more than offset Beach's flagrant support for King George in the minds of many and Beach was cut considerable slack. Moreover, the Church of England was not composed exclusively of Tories; Ridgefield libertymen such as Vivus Dauchy and Nathan Smith, for example, simply refused to change faith during the War.

When the Redding selectmen formally requested of Beach **"... that for the future you would omit praying in public that the King, George the third or any other foreign Prince, or Power, may vanquish, etc., the People of this land,"**[27] the good Reverend still refused to be silenced. Eventually soldiers filed into his church and threatened violence, but tradition tells us that Beach paid them no mind, and his quiet courage convinced the would-be attackers to stack their muskets and remain through the service. On another occasion, a musket ball purportedly sped through the church door narrowly missing the Reverend in mid sermon... but Beach never flinched! Such was the strength of his faith and the power of his personality. Until his death (apparently from natural causes) in 1782 — seven years into the War — John Beach promulgated Anglican gospel and loyalty to King George from his pulpit without retribution.

In hindsight the choice between Patriot cause and loyalty to the Crown would seem to be a "no-brainer," but in late 1776 it was a torturous decision that split Ridgefield families in half. While Josiah Stebbins and his brother Benjamin Jr., for example, remained steadfast with King George, three other brothers (Joseph, Nathan, and Samuel) embraced the Rebel position. Although fifteen local Smith men fought for the cause of independence, Jeremiah, Hezekiah, and Josiah Smith went over to the British in 1777. Brothers Lemuel and Samuel Morehouse likewise sought different camps, while prominent Loyalist and staunch Episcopal churchman Epenetus How(e) found himself married to the daughter of one of Ridgefield's foremost patriots — Vivus Dauchy. The political persuasion of local physician Dr. John Andreas has escaped history, however Loyalist pressure must have been strong because his wife was a daughter of Reverend Ingersoll and his house occupied a town-green lot two doors away from the good reverend! Keelers and Hoyts had lived next door to one another on Town Street since 1712, fought Indian Wars together and inter-married, yet they too found themselves on opposite sides when it came to Revolution.

Despite such strains, Tory and Patriot coexisted out of necessity in this interdependent agricultural community, for ties of religion, marriage, barter obligation, and simple friendship still bound neighbors together. Besides, what was one to do when the minister, miller, tanner, hatter, and blacksmith were Loyalist... and perhaps son-in-law as well? Of course, powerful forces were bearing down from all sides, but as slumbering farm fields awakened under the April sun, Ridgefielders hunkered down together... and watched... and waited.

III. The British Arrive

Had local militia Captain Timothy Benedict been watching from his Ridgebury home the windy morning of Sunday April 27, he would have seen the burnished muskets and heard the tramping feet of an army on the march. Headed directly for his crossroad domicile, and guided by none other than Josiah Stebbins, plodded a formidable British force four-abreast, cannon and all!

The previous Friday evening nearly 1,900 soldiers under the command of Major General William Tryon disembarked from fourteen Royal Navy transports off Cedar Point (present-day Westport) at the mouth of the Saugatuck River. Once ashore, they were joined by a number of Loyalist "guides," bringing the expedition to more than 2,000 men.[1] Under cover of darkness, in the face of pouring rain and strong winds, the column marched virtually unchallenged by Patriot militia directly to their objective — the inadequately protected American supply depot in Danbury — where they encamped Saturday night. As Sunday morning dawned, Tryon's army quit Danbury, having set torch to Patriot stores, along with the meeting house, nineteen dwellings, and as many as twenty-two barns and storehouses. Hoping to elude a hornet's nest of American pursuers, Tryon took a different return route to Cedar Point, and steered through Ridgebury to Ridgefield.

"The enemy left Danbury at about eight o'clock this morning"[2] wrote local intelligence agent John Field to his area commander, General Alexander McDougall in Peekskill. **"They have a number of horsemen with them, and march in great haste,"**[3] added fellow observer John

Campbell. Delayed by en-mired artillery pieces at Wolf Pond Run (now appropriately named Miry Brook) on Danbury's southwestern border, the British entered Ridgefield's Ridgebury parish sometime before ten o'clock in the morning. But was the rank and file reeling from the inevitable consequences of a night of drunkenness?

Oral tradition has it that British soldiers on the previous evening had consumed much of the **"120 puncheons of Rum [and] 30 pipes of wine"** reported to have been destroyed in Danbury according to Sir William Howe's dispatch #54 of May 22nd to Colonial Secretary Lord George Germain in London. Virtually every nineteenth-century American version of the incident perpetuates this hearsay and speculates upon the details. For example, Gideon Hollister's 1855 *History of Connecticut* described *"... a scene of drunkenness that surpasses description. Hundreds lay scattered at random wherever the palsying demon had overtaken them."*[4] Four decades later, Danbury historian James Bailey was even more graphic:

> *King George stood no chance whatever in the Presence of King Alcohol, and went down before him at once. The riot continued far into the night.... The drunken men went up and down Main Street in squads, singing army songs, shouting coarse speeches, hugging each other, swearing, yelling, and otherwise conducting themselves as becomes an invader when he is very, very drunk.*[5]

But these lurid commentaries must be considered pure patriotic poppycock. They lack an identifiable source and no eyewitness account corroborates such behavior. As might be expected, senior British officers at the scene said nothing about any such incident in their formal reports. Since the weather was wet and foul that night, and Tryon roused his men at two o'clock the following morning, there was probably little to report. British Captain Archibald Robertson's terse, unemotional diary was also blank on the subject. Soberly concluding that, "soldiers being what they are," Robert McDevitt admitted in his 1974 *British Viewpoint* that isolated incidences of drunkenness likely occurred, but that the harsh hand of military discipline prevailed among these select regiments representing the cream of British arms in North America.

McDevitt's conclusion seems well-grounded, for General Tryon's written orders not only expressly forbid plundering, but also directed the quartermaster to supply his expedition with its own libations: **"two days allowance of Rum, which the Comg [sic] Officers of Regts [sic] will take care to have mixed with water."**[6] Furthermore, Tryon's superior officer, Sir William Howe, had personally encouraged restraint in the hope that southwestern Connecticut might return to the Crown. Perhaps for this very reason, the rowdy German mercenary units known as Hessians were purposely excluded from Tryon's invasion force.

Most likely, then, the red-clad regiments trudging up the long hill from Danbury toward Timothy Benedict's Ridgebury home were perfectly sober. What's more, they were handpicked men! Sir William Howe had directed six of his most experienced regular infantry regiments to provide 250 soldiers apiece for the Danbury mission. Typical British regiments of the period[7] contained ten companies, each with captain, two lieutenants, two sergeants, three corporals and at least thirty-eight privates totaling about 460 effectives; therefore barely more than half the regimental complements were chosen for the Danbury expedition.

Most senior of the regular regiments was the 4th, or "King's Own" Regiment of Foot (Studholme Hodgson, Colonel), across whose colors strode the "lion of England" personally presented by King William III in gratitude for the Fourth's devotion to his royal person at the Battle of Boyne. Formed in 1680, the unit had also fought with distinction at Gibraltar (1704), Spain and Flanders, and bore the brunt of the Scottish attack at Culloden (1746). Bloodied at Concord and Lexington, the "King's Own" suffered more than fifty casualties at Bunker (Breed's) Hill where its light company was virtually eliminated, then participated in Howe's walkover conquest of New York. Still in service today, the unit is now known as the King's Own Royal Border Regiment.

Perhaps as rich in tradition was the 23rd Foot, or Royal Welsh Fusiliers (Nestor Balfour, Lt. Colonel), who proudly marched behind a smartly groomed regimental goat when on campaign — one officer noting in 1777 the "ancientness of the custom." Assembled in 1689 by Lord Herbert of Chirbury to serve King William III in opposing James II and his French allies, the unit's colors displayed the Prince of Wales' white ostrich plume heraldry. The Royal Welsh became the stuff of legend in the glorious Anglo-German victory at Minden (1759) as backbone of a brigade that was accidentally ordered forward, unsupported, against more than ten times its number. Heroically standing their ground without cover in an open plain, the redcoat brigade broke three lines of cavalry, putting the French to rout when the rest of the allied army came up. In America since 1773, the 23rd sustained heavy casualties at Concord, Lexington and Bunker (Breed's) Hill, then tasted victory at Long Island and White Plains. It was a prestigious unit whose titular colonel was none other than the commander-in-chief of North American British forces himself, Sir William Howe.

First mustered at Nottingham by Sir William Clifton in 1685, the East Yorkshire Riding Regiment amalgamated into the 15th Regiment of Foot in 1751. The unit contributed mightily to Britain's conquest of Canada during the Seven Years War, serving At General Wolfe's side when Quebec was wrested from France, then returned to North America in 1776 as part of William Howe's Long Island assault force. In perpetual mourning for Wolfe's heroic death on Quebec's Plains of Abraham, the gold lace of regimental officer uniforms was lined with black.

An Irish regiment informally called the "Enniskillens," the 27th Foot also fought at Quebec in 1759 during the Seven Years War. Red coats faced with bright yellow, the 44th Foot was formed thirty-six years earlier in East Essex, and proudly traced its North American service back to 1758 when the unit was all but destroyed by Native American tribesmen in General Braddock's ill-fated French and Indian War Virginia campaign. Tryon's sixth regiment, the 64th Foot (Black Knots), participated in the 1768 occupation of Boston, transferred to Halifax, returned to Boston prior to Lexington and Concord, bled at Bunker (Breed's) Hill, and shone under Colonel Alexander Leslie during the taking of Long Island.

Conventional ten-company British infantry regiments of the day contained two specialized companies — grenadiers and light companies. The former, whose tall bearskin caps and large bearing served to intimidate raw opponents, were chosen for size and strength. Adept at close-in work with bayonet, these giants traditionally occupied a position of privilege on the regimental right flank. Light companies on the opposite flank were a product of British experience in the seven-year French & Indian War, when in 1758 Lt. Colonel Thomas Gage (who would later become His Majesty's supreme commander in North America) persuaded the War Department to create a "light" regiment. This improvised unit of wiry athletic men, clad in less-formal functional uniforms, maneuvered more easily in rugged terrain and, as skilled marksmen, excelled in detached flanking duties or as skirmishers in advance of a main force. Gage's experiment proved so successful that light companies were assigned in 1771 to all Crown infantry regiments. Cocked hats contrasting sharply with grenadier bearskins and light company leather caps, the eight remaining "battalion" or "hat" companies, completed each regimental formation and constituted the rank and file of massed tactical deployments.

Tryon's infantry was supported by a splendidly garbed, formidably armed and superbly mounted subaltern's detachment of ten horse from the 17th Light Dragoons, to which was added a contingent from the 4th Royal Artillery with six three-pound field pieces. Lightweight and highly mobile, the guns had a range of 2,000 yards, but were most effective at about half that distance. Weighing no more than 700 pounds, each cannon was drawn by a three-horse team and handled by four soldiers known as "matrosses" and "wheelers," who also hauled the piece when horses or oxen were not available.

The strike force was brought to its full complement of at least 1,860 effectives by another regiment unmentioned in Tryon's written orders, the 300-strong Prince of Wales Loyal American Volunteers. One of more than *forty* Loyalist regiments — the American Revolution's best-kept secret — to fight for King George, the Prince of Wales Volunteers were mostly Connecticut men. Induced by a £5 bounty, up to 100 acres of Mississippi land plus pay, quarters, clothing and arms, these Connecticut Loyalists were commanded by former Royal Governor of the Bahamas Montfort Browne. Only four days earlier Browne's regiment had mustered for the first time, boasting 595 officers, sergeants, and rank and file; but only about half were selected for the Danbury mission.[8]

Montfort Browne first appeared on the North American scene in 1768 as lieutenant governor of West Florida. Appointed governor of the Bahamas a year later, Browne embarrassed the Crown in early 1776 by surrendering his command to a ragtag eight-vessel Continental fleet under Commodore Esek Hopkins. Although Browne knew of the American expedition, he had made no effort to defend the islands and relinquished his fort upon demand, along with an impressive amount of stores, cannon and shot. As one historian put it, "The Americans had conquered merely by coming."[9]

Confined to house arrest in Middletown, Connecticut as a prisoner-of-war, Montfort Browne smuggled a letter to Sir William Howe immodestly proposing to raise a 4000-man brigade of Connecticut Loyalists right under Patriot noses. Howe rose to the challenge and quickly exchanged captured American major general William Alexander (the self-anointed "Lord" Stirling) for Browne, then commissioned him colonel of a provincial regiment — provided he could actually raise one! After saturating Connecticut with recruiting broadsides, Browne commandeered Norwalk Tory Jesse Hoyt's sloop to gather-up volunteer clusters at clandestine meeting spots along the sound. Within six months enough Connecticut men mustered at his Flushing headquarters to form the Prince of Wales Loyal American Volunteers. Tryon's Danbury expedition would be the unit's baptism under fire.

Wearing the green tunic and white breeches of Browne's Provincials was a freshly commissioned 2nd Lieutenant hailing from Ridgefield whom we met earlier — Josiah Stebbins. His tanning/shoemaking business had collapsed under Patriot boycott as **"an enemy to the liberties of America"** and he absconded in October to White Plains, where his French-and-Indian-War experience evidently parlayed entree to British arms. Granted a warrant by Browne to raise a company of Fairfield County volunteers, Stebbins undoubtedly viewed Tryon's foray as an unparalleled recruiting opportunity and perhaps occasion to square a few old scores by musket and torch. The martial exuberance of Stebbins and his ilk delighted Colonel Browne, who later gushed to Lord George Germain:

> **... their undaunted behavior and resolution, astonished every officer of the expedition. They could scarce be restrained, often advancing musket shot before any other Corps. But nothing was more pleasing, ... than that of paying not the least attention or partiality to their own Rebel relations and neighbors, who they met in numbers of both sexes, and to whom they expressed upon all occasions a resentment for not joining in fighting for the best of Kings.**[10]

His Majesty's Chain of Command

Well-born third son of Charles Tryon of Bulwick Hall, expedition leader William Tryon was an undistinguished officer of the parade-ground variety who had married well (the influential Margaret Wake and her £30,000 estate) and parlayed family political influence into a successful career in Imperial service. His father's money produced a lieutenant's commission in the prestigious Foot Guards in 1751; lieutenant-colonelcy followed seven year later without Tryon having seen any real action. Appointed lieutenant governor of North Carolina Colony in 1764, Tryon was assured by Board of Trade president Lord Hillsborough (his wife's relative) that governorship would soon follow. Within a year North Carolina Governor Dobbs obligingly departed this earth and Hillsborough proved as good as his word. Then in 1771, after demonstrating his sternness in dealing with unruly Carolina provincials, Tryon was appointed royal governor of New York Province. At the outbreak of Revolution Governor Tryon, like most British leaders, assigned the unrest to a handful of Rebel ringleaders and threatened to burn any New York committeeman's house within his reach, while "offering twenty silver dollars for every acting committeeman who should be delivered up to the King's troops."[11]

"**The man is generous, good-natured, and no doubt brave, but weak and vain to an extreme degree,**" observed one New York Loyalist about William Tryon.[12] To be fair, the controversial Tryon was also an able administrator who tried to balance advancement of the colonies with unswerving devotion to his king. Faithful husband and hardworking governor, Tryon possessed many positive characteristics, but humility and restraint were not among them. Even Loyalist Reverend John Vardill admitted **"tho a Gentleman of Integrity & Fortitude, [Tryon] was made by his *Vanity* a dupe to every flattering Imposter."**[13] His Honor's good nature and fortitude, if not bravery, were severely tested in October 1775 when the Continental Congress determined to introduce Tryon (a la New Jersey Governor William Franklin) to a Patriot prison. Smoking out potential arrest, the "Governor" adroitly shifted office aboard *Duchess of Gordon* in New York harbor under the guns of His Majesty's warship *Asia* until Howe's conquest of Long Island returned some terra firma to govern.

His own significance eclipsed by Howe's military superintendence of New York, the fifty-two-year-old William Tryon imagined a grander role for himself — Loyalist military commander — in the unfolding drama for possession of New York, New Jersey and Connecticut. Whether driven by bravery or vanity, Tryon made no secret of his ambition to return to the King's arms, and as early as January 1776 London's old-boy-network buzzed with his scheme:

> He [Tryon] seems positive of being able to raise two thousand men, upon the arrival of the army in New York, who may be rendered very useful if accompanied by his personal services in the field."[14]

Although his personal request (through private channels) to King George III for a regular regimental colonelcy had long fallen on deaf royal ears, Tryon successfully petitioned William Howe for a military role in the upcoming 1777 campaign. Brevetted major general of provincials by Howe, Tryon gained command of New York's Loyalist battalions, but smarted at his inferior status **"behind all the Major Generals in this army though I am an older colonel than any of them."**[15]

In the wake of George Washington's surprising success at Trenton, Tryon had earlier written directly to Colonial

Secretary Lord Germain on New Year's Eve 1776 requesting active military duty. After over-optimistically promising Germain that **"A majority of the inhabitants of the Connecticut river are firm friends of the government"**, Tryon concluded his missive with a none-too-subtle reference to the Trenton embarrassment: **"I trust this tarnish to the campaign, will in due season be wiped away by some brilliant enterprise of the King's forces, who entertain the keenest sense of the insult."**[16]

Was the governor suggesting a Connecticut venture to square His Majesty's account, with none other but himself at the head? Could Tryon's saber rattling have pre-disposed Germain to bless Howe's Danbury initiative four months later? Indeed, James Murray's *History of the War in America* (London: 1778, Vol.2, p. 239) credits Tryon as expedition brainchild, and six personal letters between November 30th, 1776 and January 7, 1777 show Tryon clearly had Germain's ear. Furthermore, Germain and King George III officially approved Tryon's appointment as major general of provincials that spring, and on April 22, 1777 he was confirmed by Sir William Howe to head the secret Danbury raid.

Perhaps because Tryon was Lord Germain's choice and not his own, Howe also assigned Brigadier General Sir William "Woolly" Erskine, a tested combat leader and quartermaster-general of the British Army in North America, to accompany the expedition. Erskine, who had previously incurred substantial Rebel casualties in a successful New Jersey foraging expedition, was undoubtedly responsible for the mission's success; even Tryon admitted in his own final report to Germain that **"...without him I should have been much embarrassed, if nothing worse."**[17] In fact, Captain Robertson observed in his own diary that: **"Great praise is due to Sir William Erskine for his good conduct on this Expedition. Tho' General Tryon and Brigadier General Agnew were older, He ordered everything."**[18]

Robertson was wrong about Erskine's relative youth; in fact Sir William was actually a year older than Tryon. What's more he was every inch the experienced field officer Tryon was not. An Edinburgh Scot, sixteen-year-old Erskine had joined the elite mounted Scot's Greys in 1743, won battlefield promotion to cornet against the French at Fontenoy, and earned his lieutenant-colonelcy in 1762. A year later Erskine was knighted by King George after presenting the Crown with sixteen enemy banners captured by his regiment on the fields of Germany. Made brigadier general and assigned to North America in 1776, Sir William commanded the 7th brigade in William Howe's conquest of Long Island.

Howe backed up the universally respected and well liked Erskine with two other proven professionals. Forty-four-year-old James Agnew had arrived in Boston in 1775 as lieutenant colonel of the aforementioned 44th Foot. Promoted to brigadier general in the aftermath of Lexington and Concord, Agnew successfully commanded a brigade in the British victory at Long Island, and led the 4th, 15th and 23rd regiments on the road to Ridgefield. The 27th, 44th, and 64th Foot were brigaded under the experienced professional eye of Lieutenant Colonel John Maxwell, a personal choice of General Erskine.

As for Robertson, the thirty-nine-year-old captain-lieutenant of Royal Corps of Engineers had served in America as early as 1767 and was assigned to Howe's Boston command in November 1775. Since few reliable inland maps of the colonies existed in the British folio, Robertson undoubtedly accompanied the Danbury mission for survey purposes, indeed producing a topographical sketch of the raid that his superior, Captain John Montresor, reproduced in map form shortly afterwards. If his diary is any clue to Robertson's persona, the man must have been of objective temper and thorough competence.

Third son of Viscount George Howe and commander-in-chief of His Majesty's North American ground force, Sir William Howe was a distant relative of King George III — his mother was illegitimately sired by George I. After entering the army in 1740 at the age of seventeen (what else was a third-born son to do?), the coarse, burly, dark-complexioned Howe had emerged as one of Britain's most distinguished junior officers, known for both physical courage and his size. Barely thirty, Howe had led the advance guard assault as lieutenant colonel of the 58th Foot in James Wolfe's stirring victory over Marquis de Montcalm at Quebec in 1759. Sixteen years later, Major General Howe, as second in command to Thomas Gage at Bunker Hill, personally directed the redcoat line's three assaults, his uniform spattered with the blood of fallen staff officers. After replacing Gage as Commander-in-Chief, Howe then evacuated the British Army from Boston and outgeneraled George Washington to capture Long Island and New York.

Sir William (his Long Island conquest rewarded by knighthood) was a sitting Member of Parliament who prior to hostilities had publicly informed his constituents he would not fight the colonists under any circumstances. When directed to America by Lord George Germain, Howe inquired whether the communiqué was a request or an order, setting sail only after being advised it was the latter. Genuinely moved by a memorial erected by the colonists in honor of his older brother George's death (in the arms of Connecticut's Israel Putnam) at Fort Ticonderoga during the French and Indian conflict, Howe was reluctant to treat the colonial populace harshly. Even Sir William's officers questioned his leniency.[9] Why, some asked, were Rebel soldiers allowed to return unmolested to their Long Island homes after the island was invested? And why were captured Rebel officers allowed to walk the streets on parole in uniform, or exchanged as prisoners, rather than hung as traitors to the Crown? **"Not one Rebel,"** lamented the diary of one King's officer, **"has suffered death yet, except in Action."**[19]

Perhaps because he sincerely believed most Americans would eventually return to their senses and embrace British rule, Howe, until he resigned his command in 1778, treated the Rebels more like naughty cousins than true enemies. Less generous observers assigned this recalcitrance to indecision, alcohol, or Howe's well-known affair with Mrs. Joshua Loring (a Loyalist commissary's wife), but acerbic social gadfly Horace Walpole, suspecting Sir William's heart was never in the affair, allowed: **"Howe was one of those brave, silent brothers, and was reckoned sensible, though so silent that nobody knew whether he was or not."**[20]

Howe's superior, Lord Germain (George Sackville) was truly an "odd duck." Despite an effeminate manner that generated whispers of homosexuality, the third-born son of Lord Dorset received his military commission in 1740 and served with distinction in the War of the Austrian Succession, only to be drummed out of the service during the Seven Years War! While commanding British cavalry in service of Prince Ferdinand of Brunswick against the French at Minden in 1759, Sackville either would not, or could not, give the order for his troops to advance in support of the allied assault. Subsequently court-martialed and branded unfit to serve the Crown (averting execution by only three votes), Sackville was dismissed from service under the stench of cowardice. Furthermore, King George II ordered a statement of Sackville's military unsuitability read aloud to every single British regiment! Within a year, however, George II was dead, succeeded by his insecure twenty-two-year-old grandson George III. Overtly rejecting his grandfather's politics, the callow new monarch surrounded himself with pliable men who had fallen out of favor with the prior regime, and Sackville was slowly rehabilitated through a series of minor appointments and parliamentary service. By 1775, Sackville (now Lord Germain) had risen to minister of American affairs because his newfound backbone and consistent hard-line approach on colonial issues reflected George III's own mindset. One can only imagine what proud, tight-lipped, combat-proven career-officer Sir William Howe must have thought about taking direction from a convicted coward.

Having been introduced to the British command team, a few words are in order about His Majesty's officer corps. While Generals could only be "made" by the War Department at Whitehall, and regimental colonelcy was a prize political plum of the Crown, junior officers purchased their commissions and their promotions, whether secured on the battlefield or the backroom of a gentleman's club. A captaincy might cost £1,000 while the market price for a lieutenant colonelcy approached £3,500, provided the suitor (and his well-placed supporters) prevailed over sometimes stiff competition for the colonel's personal approval. In the case of a unit raised by the King himself, such as the 4th Regiment of Foot, these commissions were paid to the Crown. Other regiments, such as the 23rd Foot, had been raised by well-heeled individuals who, having gained the Secretary of War's ear (or purse), purchased the colonelcy and pocketed commission fees from all regimental officers. In such cases, day-to-day command duties were usually delegated to a lieutenant colonel or major, freeing the colonel for other political or military adventure. Sir William Howe, for example, advanced far beyond mere regimental rank, but still retained colonelcy of his 23rd Foot and whatever commission fees that flowed from its thirty-two-officer complement. Of course, Howe had long since relegated regimental operating responsibilities to personally chosen junior officers.

Consequently His Majesty's army was commanded by very wealthy men from "quality" families, or at the very least with superior connections to the ruling aristocracy. Even the lowliest subaltern might be third or fourth son of a prominent aristocrat and carry an impressive hereditary title, but most junior officers came from modest upper middle-class families. Lacking resources to rise to top rank, these men devoted themselves to regiment and profession. Frederick Mackenzie of the Royal Welsh Fusiliers (23rd Foot) provides a typical example. Son of a Dublin merchant, Mackenzie was commissioned a lieutenant in 1745, but could not purchase his captaincy until the fall of 1775 in Boston — a span of thirty years! King George's generals were mostly scions of "quality," but Mackenzie and his peers, such as Major Henry Hope of the 44th Foot and Captain William Hutchinson of the 27th Foot, formed the backbone of a proud, disciplined professional army.

Officers were not hard to come by, given the profusion of upper-class second-and-third-born sons with time on their hands; the real problem was finding men to command. An army career was unpopular with the middle classes, and King and Parliament dared not press men into the army, unlike the navy, for the country would not have stood for it. The service obligation of twenty years (reduced to the duration in wartime) didn't help either! As a result, regimental ranks consisted of the most impoverished souls to whom meager pay of less than £4 a year after equipment deductions represented the best if not only option. Others enlisted barely one step ahead of the law for once in King's service they were safe from civil authority. In wartime, prison cells might even be emptied for regimental fodder although the worst of the lot were posted to the Caribbean where disease commuted their sentences. These rascals represented the absolute dregs of British society and were kept in line by a ferocious punishment regimen, in which 500 lashes for insolence to an officer, or even 1,000 lashes, were not uncommon. A plethora of lesser sentences included running the gauntlet, clubbing, booting, or "bottling" the unfortunate offender in a small box. Desertion was punishable by death.

In truth, North American-based British officers often had more in common with Patriot merchants and yeoman farmers than with their own soldiers. As we shall later discover, if oral tradition is to be believed, individual Crown officers often demonstrated real civility during their uninvited Ridgefield visit. Despite his strong pro-American bias, even James Case's 1927 account (pages 16 & 17) allowed the polite treatment of Anna Crossman in Compo and Mrs. Thankful Bradley of Weston when they inadvertently confronted British troops on the march.

Tryon himself was cordial with the country people, reputedly alighting from horseback to share a cup of milk or other refreshment en route to Danbury. Near Weston, upon learning a lady had been robbed of a dress by one of his troops, he restored her garment and punished the offender on the spot.[21] To be sure, Tryon had little sympathy for Rebels and would have savored opportunity to torch ringleader homes, but he was under Sir William Howe's order to behave with restraint in hope the countryside would flock like so many sheep to the safety of British arms. Therefore no committeeman homestead was burned en route to Danbury, not even the Redding residence of fiercely patriotic Lieutenant Stephen Betts, who was physically dragged from his own hearth as a prisoner. If fired upon, however, British gentility would of course be quickly abandoned.

Tryon Vacates Danbury

Confident of his superior martial strength, Tryon apparently intended to give his men the next day (Sunday) to rest in Danbury, but a reliable Loyalist source provided alarming news just before midnight that 1,500 Americans were in his rear. In reality only six hundred Connecticut militia troops under General David Wooster were in position to cut off the British retreat, but another 421 men of Colonel

Henry Ludington's Dutchess County, New York militia, together with hundreds of Goshen, Litchfield and Woodbury minutemen were on their way. General Alexander McDougall dispatched 1200 Continentals from Peekskill, and somewhere in the woods outside of Danbury lurked Colonel Jedediah Huntington and fifty Continental troops of the 1st Connecticut Line, accompanied by 100-or-so militia with which he was supposed to have defended the depot. Perhaps most disturbing of all, General Benedict Arnold, respected for ardor under fire and ability to draw men to his flag, was rumored to be with Wooster.

Upon receiving such serious news, Tryon awakened his men at two a.m. and according to Robertson at **"daybreak set fire to all the stores and march'd about 8 o'clock."**[22] After feinting toward the Hudson in an attempt to confuse his pursuers, Tryon put his column in motion toward Ridgefield. Prince of Wales Loyalist Volunteers in the vanguard, sandwiching more than twenty Patriot prisoners taken from Redding, Weston and Danbury, the redcoat column executed a four-mile traverse to Ridgebury center. (See *Figure Five* on page 51.)   Just east of Ridgebury, a flanking force peeled to the south on a no-longer-existing wood-road through a section called "Bogus," while the bulk of Tryon's army filed through the tiny hamlet.

> *First came a body of light horsemen, then three pieces of cannon, followed by the main body...with three pieces of cannon in their rear. As they passed the house of Capt. Timothy Benedict, standing on the corner of the road leading to Danbury, they fired two pistol shots at some person looking out at a window, but without doing any harm. As the light horsemen passed through the outskirts of the village, they fired at several persons near the New York state line.*[23]

Hearsay has embellished the Benedict House incident to include a fair young girl who dodged a shower of bullets (see Case, p. 32) at an upstairs window. This incident smacks of patriotic embroidery, but clearly something untoward took place, for a reimbursement request for more than £10 appears under Timothy Benedict's name on a town damages summary document later submitted to the General Assembly.

Unlike the Benedict house most dwellings near the little crossroads were deserted. Because Fairfield County militia commander Silliman (alerted two weeks earlier by Governor Trumbull of a potential Danbury raid) dispatched nightriders Paul-Revere-like throughout the countryside when the British bogeyman actually materialized, most Ridgebury residents had already moved prize possessions into hiding. Observing Danbury in flames, the residents packed whatever else they could carry into carts and like tavern-owner Abraham Rockwell hid in the woods, or fled to a hill a mile or so northwest of the present Congregational Church[24] and watched the enemy parade through their parish.

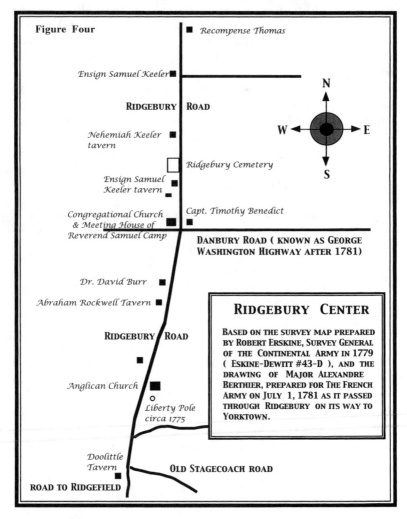

Figure Four

Recompense Thomas

Ensign Samuel Keeler

RIDGEBURY ROAD

N
W ← → E
S

Nehemiah Keeler
tavern

Ridgebury Cemetery

Ensign Samuel
Keeler tavern

Congregational Church
& Meeting House of
Reverend Samuel Camp

Capt. Timothy Benedict

**DANBURY ROAD (KNOWN AS GEORGE
WASHINGTON HIGHWAY AFTER 1781)**

Dr. David Burr

Abraham Rockwell Tavern

RIDGEBURY ROAD

Anglican Church

Liberty Pole
circa 1775

RIDGEBURY CENTER

BASED ON THE SURVEY MAP PREPARED
BY ROBERT ERSKINE, SURVEY GENERAL
OF THE CONTINENTAL ARMY IN 1779
(ESKINE-DEWITT #43-D), AND THE
DRAWING OF MAJOR ALEXANDRE
BERTHIER, PREPARED FOR THE FRENCH
ARMY ON JULY 1, 1781 AS IT PASSED
THROUGH RIDGEBURY ON ITS WAY TO
YORKTOWN.

Doolittle
Tavern

OLD STAGECOACH ROAD

ROAD TO RIDGEFIELD

Leaving Ridgebury center in their wake, the main British column turned south on Ridgebury Road, passed the still-standing Rockwell Inn, old Episcopal Church (knocked down in 1810), Ichabod Doolittle's Tavern, and then navigated a gap through the Asproom Ledges. Perhaps His Majesty's minions helped themselves to the liquor supply in Abraham Rockwell's vacated roadside tavern, for Rockwell later claimed more than £16 in damages (See Appendix C). More serious damage was inflicted on the property of outspoken Congregationalist minister Samuel Camp. And if the roadside liberty pole erected by Ridgebury Patriots in '75 were still standing, Montfort Browne's Loyalist vanguard would have surely cut it down. To the west a flanking party skirted the New York border to screen the column from any potential American thrust down the North Salem Road.

Along the northeast side of Lake Mamanasquag (Mamanasco), where Buffalo Creek flowed out below North Salem Road, stood the gristmill of Isaac Keeler. Having taken Benjamin Stebbins' daughter Hannah as his second wife, Isaac Keeler was in fact brother-in-law to Josiah Stebbins, the local Tory who marched with the British column. Informed the mill was a Patriot storehouse, Tryon's flanking party burned the building and its contents — 50 to 100 barrels of flour and a quantity of Indian corn. One wonders, however, if Keeler's mill was truly a military storage center, or whether Tory neighbors Daniel Sherwood and David Burt, together with Josiah Stebbins, simply used the occasion as an opportunity to settle old scores.

Twelve-year-old Lizzie Hunt looked up from her play and watched in awe as the red-clad regiments descended Ridgebury Hill into the school district dubbed "Scotland" in honor of the area's prolific Scott family. Family papers vividly recall that:

> ...she and other children ran down to the bank of the road to watch their advance. She watched them roll out the barrels of flour and set fire to them and the mill itself, and heard the explosions as the bungs shot out with a noise like gunfire. It was for this very reason, according to this source, that this section of the Scotland District became known as Bungtown.[25]

Perhaps half a mile south of the burning mill, the column halted for a late breakfast on the flats below Scotland District schoolhouse. Scott family papers describe the scene:

> *The British also captured and killed cattle for their men; one cow evaded capture by running into the lake and drowning... Several of the British officers called at the house of Nathan Scott and asked to borrow knives and forks with which to cut the meat...and when the British had finished using them, they returned them to their owners.*[26]

Local tradition asserts that the aforementioned cattle were plundered from Ridgebury farmers by redcoat foragers, but more likely the beasts had accompanied Tryon's men from Danbury. **"They have with them five ox teams, fifty or sixty cattle, and the same number of sheep,"**[27] wrote Patriot informant John Campbell earlier that morning in his eyewitness report to General McDougall about British movements from Danbury. If Campbell is to be believed (and there is no reason why he shouldn't), His Majesty's soldiers were likely supplied with plundered Danbury depot stores and therefore innocent of civilian livestock theft in Ridgefield.

Having marched continuously, often in wind and rain, carrying a fourteen pound musket and another forty-five pounds in knapsack and haversack since commencing operations eleven o'clock Friday evening, the rank and file must have collapsed in a tired heap around their hastily assembled Sunday meal site. The freshly butchered beef was a temporary treat to be savored while standard-issue "Brown Bess" muskets were stacked and canteens replenished. Since no real resistance had yet been offered from the Americans, pickets, if posted at all, were likely drawn in.

IV. The Patriots Strike!

While British soldiers chewed on fresh-killed Connecticut beef, the Rebels were executing a plan hatched in nearby Bethel late the previous evening. As ranking officer, sixty-six-year-old militia Major General David Wooster would take several hundred of his now 700-man force[1] to harass Tryon's rear. The objective was to buy time for militia General Gold Selleck Silliman and Continental Brigadier General Benedict Arnold to speed toward Ridgefield with the remaining troops and prepare a defensive position before the British arrived. Together the Patriot trio envisioned a pincer movement that just might stall their enemy until overwhelming reinforcements could arrive.

In April 1777, David Wooster (Yale '39) was the ranking brigadier general and, based on seniority, the third ranking general officer in the Continental army. His military career began as lieutenant of the sloop *Defense* guarding the Connecticut coast in 1741 and he was made captain the following year. Wooster's performance eight years later during the British siege and capture of Louisburg in French Canada earned him a regular British Army commission — rare privilege for a colonial! Acknowledging his four campaigns as regimental colonel of militia in the French and Indian Wars, the Connecticut legislature appointed Wooster major general of state forces immediately after word of Lexington and Concord. Still on half-pay as a commissioned British captain of the 51st Foot, he was then appointed in June 1775 by the Continental Congress as one of eight brigadiers to command the Continental Line.

Wooster was unable to take Quebec with an under-sized force in the summer of 1776; the mission ended in disaster and he was formally charged with incapacity — a polite synonym for incompetence.   Demanding an investigation by Congress, the aging general was subsequently acquitted of blame, thereby retaining his Continental commission. Having lost George Washington's support due to perceived incompetence, his Continental career was over, but in a vote of confidence, Connecticut renewed Wooster's appointment as major general of militia in October 1776, and gave him command of three of the state's six militia brigades.

Spring 1777 found Wooster and his Connecticut militia on defensive duty along the "neutral ground" at New Rochelle, just inside Westchester County. But his overly cautious retreat from British probes precipitated a personal letter of disappointment from General Washington himself:

> **I was a good deal surprised to find yours [letter] of the 6 [March] dated from Rye, supposing there was a real necessity of your retreating from New Rochelle, you certainly might have returned immediately... All accounts from your quarters complain loudly of this retreat as a most injudicious step.[2]**

Smarting from His Excellency's rebuke, the sixty-six-year-old Wooster had repaired to the comfort of home in New Haven. News from Fairfield that Tryon had landed at Cedar Point represented a last opportunity to restore his reputation, so the old warhorse gathered his aides and began the brutal thirty-mile horseback trek from New Haven to southwestern Connecticut late the rainy evening of Friday, April 25th.

Also in New Haven was perhaps the most perplexing and enigmatic figure of the American Revolution — Benedict Arnold.   Great-grandson of Rhode Island Colony's second colonial governor, Arnold had long struggled to repair the family's deteriorated finances and accompanying fall from highest social rank. The upwardly mobile Arnold parlayed a profitable Caribbean smuggling trade (as did congressional president John Hancock) into a respectable New Haven merchant business and then secured captaincy of the 2nd

Company of Connecticut Governor Fitch's prestigious Foot Guards.

At the outbreak of hostilities, Arnold rushed his troop to the Boston siege where as one of the few uniformed units his company caught the eye of the Massachusetts Provincial command team. Commissioned by Massachusetts to commandeer the enemy artillery at Fort Ticonderoga, Arnold shared with Ethan Allen and his Green Mountain boys in the glorious capture of Ticonderoga. After being appointed colonel at General Washington's urging, Arnold next garnered widespread acclaim as "the American Hannibal" by marching to Quebec across 350 miles of brutal winter wilderness terrain. Wounded in the Quebec assault of New Year's Eve 1775, he was subsequently promoted to brigadier general by a grateful Congress. Put in charge of matters on Lake Champlain, the indefatigable Arnold built a makeshift fleet from scratch, the courageous sacrifice of which at Valcour Island in October 1776 temporarily saved the American garrison at Ticonderoga. After the British seized Newport in December, Arnold was made second in command of the Rhode Island defense, but in March 1777 he was aghast to hear from General Washington that Congress had promoted five less-accomplished brigadiers — all his junior — to major general.

April 1777 found Arnold on leave in New Haven preparing to confront Congress over this slight on his honor, or resign his commission, or both. Arnold had real cause for disappointment, for although lacking in political finesse, his combat record was second to none. Tryon's incursion presented an irresistible chance to trump the political issue with yet another battlefield promotion so, followed by his great friend and protégé, Lt. Colonel Eleazar Oswald (who commanded the New Haven companies of Colonel John Lamb's Second Regiment of Continental artillery), General Arnold sped toward Danbury to join fellow Masonic Lodge brother David Wooster in rendezvous with General Silliman at Redding, then pressed on to Bethel in Tryon's wake.

Exactly how Arnold accommodated himself with Wooster at Bethel is one of history's secrets, for the pair were oil and water. In the wake of Lexington and Concord, Arnold had mobilized his New Haven troop for an immediate march to Boston's aid, but was denied access to the local powder magazine by then-colonel David Wooster. Although New Haven's town fathers over-ruled Wooster, Arnold no doubt resented the aging general's hesitancy. And it was Wooster who succeeded Arnold in command at Quebec, only to be drummed out of the Continental army for incapacity and branded as a dull indecisive leader while the mercurial Benedict Arnold's star (and reputation with General Washington) was on the rise. Any Continental officer would have bristled at taking orders from a more senior militia officer and none was more jealous of his position than Arnold, so he undoubtedly pushed hard for an independent command. Although there were sound military reasons for dividing the heavily outnumbered American force in Bethel, both generals were likely happy to be rid of one another.

Gold Selleck Silliman was in a delicate position. As brigadier general of militia for Connecticut's Southwest Department, he reported directly to Wooster. Since Continental commissions prevailed over state appointments of the same grade, he was therefore junior to Arnold. What's more, even though Silliman was warned two weeks earlier about a potential Danbury raid, he had disappointed Governor Jonathan Trumbull by letting five-and-a-half valuable hours slip away, for some unexplainable reason, before notifying his superiors of the British presence off Cedar Point. Now, for reasons of military protocol, Silliman was forced to turn over his Fairfield militia to the interloper from New Haven, Benedict Arnold.

Silliman appears to have been a good-natured, public-spirited citizen whose family concerns were much on his mind — the kind of man who is a peacetime community pillar, but often devoured by impersonal fortune of war. Groomed early to follow in his father's footsteps as an influential Fairfield politician (father Ebenezer was a state senator, speaker of the General Assembly and for twenty-three years a state superior court judge), Gold Silliman's early military career was pre-arranged.[3] He began as a major in 1774 and had advanced to full colonel within a year. His well-equipped mounted unit galloped to Boston in response to the Lexington alarm, and when the British abandoned Boston for New York, Silliman was ordered south to participate in the defense.

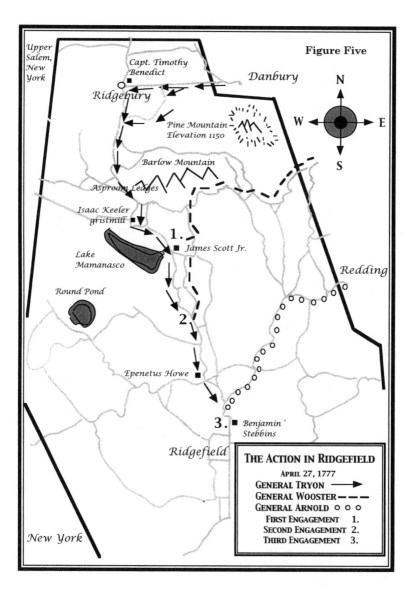

Figure Five

Upper Salem, New York

Capt. Timothy Benedict

Danbury

Ridgebury

Pine Mountain Elevation 1150

N
W — E
S

Barlow Mountain

Asproom Ledges

Isaac Keeler gristmill

1.

James Scott Jr.

Lake Mamanasco

Round Pond

Redding

2

Epenetus Howe

3.

Benjamin Stebbins

Ridgefield

New York

THE ACTION IN RIDGEFIELD

APRIL 27, 1777

GENERAL TRYON ⟶
GENERAL WOOSTER ‒ ‒ ‒
GENERAL ARNOLD ○ ○ ○
FIRST ENGAGEMENT 1.
SECOND ENGAGEMENT 2.
THIRD ENGAGEMENT 3.

By saving most of his encircled command from certain capture during Washington's retreat from New York in September, 1776, and performing honorably at White Plains the following month, Silliman was rewarded with a year-end appointment to general of the reorganized Connecticut state militia, with responsibility for Fairfield County. When he found himself in Bethel the rainy night of April 26th, Gold Silliman's reputation was at its peak, but he had neither the commanding personality of Arnold, nor the deep experience of Wooster.

The First Engagement

Fifteen-year-old Jonathan Nickerson of Ridgefield was already a full-year veteran in the Continental Army Quartermaster establishment at Danbury when he received word the British had landed off Cedar Point.[4] Nickerson proceeded to his Danbury post, but finding the town already in enemy hands, fell in with General Wooster's force somewhere between Danbury and Bethel parish.

Perhaps 300 strong after separating from Arnold, Wooster's contingent included the handful of New Haven men who had accompanied him south, a party of the 4th Westchester Militia under Major Thaddeus Crane of Upper Salem, plus about 100 effectives (many still unarmed) from the Danbury-based 16th Connecticut Militia commanded by Colonel Joseph Platt Cooke. Perhaps Danbury's wealthiest merchant, Cooke sat in the state General Assembly and was on Governor Trumbull's Council of Safety when Tryon came calling. His Danbury residence (later valued at more than £950) torched at dawn by the departing British column, Cooke evidently remained with Colonel Jedediah Huntington to secure his hometown while the bulk of his regiment, temporarily commanded by Major Nehemiah Beardsley, linked up with Wooster.

Also with Wooster was a company of Wilton Parish militia that found its way through wind and rain to Bethel the previous evening. Led by Lieutenant Seth Abbott, their ranks included sixteen-year-old Joseph Jessup, Thaddeus Sterling, Samuel St. John, Ezra Gregory, and at least ten others. Somewhere in the patchwork American aggregation were Nehemiah Keeler, a Ridgebury tavern operator who the previous month had enlisted in Captain Knowles Sears Company of Beardsley's regiment, and Ensign Hugh Cain, the Ridgefielder who operated a well-known fulling mill on the Norwalk River a few miles to the southeast.

As Wooster's eclectic and poorly armed command prepared to move out in pursuit of Tryon, reinforcements and ammunition arrived! A troop of Litchfield militia led by Captains Samuel Seymour and Eaton Jones had marched hard through the night in response to the Danbury alarm. The *Boston Gazette* of May 5th informs us of another fresh contingent from the Bay State:

> 10:00 Sunday, Wooster was joined by 140 Continental troops from Massachusetts, under Lt. Colonel Smith, but without any ammunition; happily however, there soon arrived 2000 cartridges from Peeks Kill, upon which a disposition was made to harass the enemy.

After doling out the precious cartridges, Wooster's beefed-up force worked its way down from Bethel, rushed over a rudimentary trail along Barlow Mountain's southern slope, and burst through the trees into the flat just in front of the old Scotland District schoolhouse (today's Scotland school) as the British rear guard was finishing its meal. (*Figure Five.*) With the advantage of complete surprise, the Rebels slammed into Tryon's rear-guard encampment just north of James Scott Jr.'s house, killing at least two, and capturing a number of the dazed foe. Several period accounts claimed forty prisoners were taken, but Colonel Huntington only reported twelve or thirteen in his following-day report[5] to immediate superior, General Alexander McDougall in Peekskill. Since Sir William Howe's formal returns, printed in the London press the following month, listed only twenty-nine men missing for the entire campaign, Huntington's estimate is probably closer to the mark. Ten of Howe's missing soldiers were from a single regiment, — the 23rd Foot — so most likely these Royal Welsh Fusiliers constituted that day's rear guard. Whatever his prisoner-count, Wooster promptly withdrew into the woods to plot his next move.

No more than a minor harassment, this incident failed to disrupt the British movement toward Ridgefield less than three miles distant. The two redcoat casualties were *"hastily buried in a sand-knoll north of Mr. Zalmon Main's,"* [6] and the column moved on. The unfortunate pair was incorrectly referred to as "Hessians" well into the twentieth century, but Tryon's own records clearly indicate no hired German mercenary units accompanied his expedition. Instead, the buried men were most likely British grenadiers, whose tall hats with metal plates and black-faced dress coats resembled period Hessian military garb. Almost a century later, in 1872, Dr. Archibald Y. Paddock uncovered the two skeletons while clearing the sand bank. According to Ridgefield historian Richard Venus: "One was almost perfect and was placed on exhibit at the Centennial Celebration in Philadelphia in 1876 by Doctor Paddock."[7]

Slowly, local residents emerged from hiding as the redcoats vanished down North Salem Road toward Ridgefield. One farmwife, from whom Crown officers had earlier borrowed flatware, was not, according to tradition, about to let the remains of the British bovine breakfast go to waste:

After the skirmish, and when everything had quieted down, Mrs. Nathan Scott, the grandmother of Mr. Wade, gathered up enough fat and bones to make two barrels of soap.[8]

The Second Engagement

Wooster followed Tryon's column for about an hour, waiting for the right opportunity to strike again. Somewhat more than a mile south of the first engagement, the British rearguard, anticipating another American assault, halted on some rising ground to position the trio of cannon Tryon had detailed to his rear. Wooster spotted an opportunity to capture one artillery piece and urged his men forward, but exposed no longer to the element of surprise, the rearguard wheeled and unleashed a volley that brought down the aging Patriot general's horse and easily broke his raw troops.

Before following Wooster and his wavering command back into action, a little background about the local militia is appropriate. As early as 1637, all colonists aged sixteen to sixty were ordered by the Crown to take military training in regimental drill at least two days each year. Virtually every Connecticut community implemented His Majesty's wish by forming "train bands" whose ranks typically included a captain, lieutenant, ensign, four sergeants, and sixty-four soldiers. (In 1727 the Hartford General Assembly formally established Ridgefield's militia and named Samuel St. John as captain.) Providing women opportunity to visit and townsfolk occasion to feast, these irregular trainbands commandeered village-greens across the colony for muster, drill, and consumption of rum. During the French and Indian Wars many train bands hardened into true militia, and early in the Revolution Connecticut's best-organized militia companies evolved into regiments of the Continental Line. In October 1776 the General Assembly re-organized its remaining militia into six brigades containing twenty-eight regiments. (*Figure Six* on page 56.) Of course, these irregular units were always at the governor's disposal to assist Continental forces for three-to-six-month stints, but after 1778 functioned mostly inside Connecticut's boundaries in response to British alarms such as at Danbury.

    One of the Revolution's great myths is that American irregulars were "Daniel Boone" types who could shoot the eye out of a squirrel from several hundred yards. Yes, frontier riflemen from west of the Alleghenies, such as the heralded regiment of Daniel Morgan, did indeed wield grooved-bore long rifles that were murderous from such range, but such rifle companies were a minority. Muskets of the day were smoothbore, which meant musket balls rattled down the gun-barrel after discharge and might exit at most any angle. One eccentric Patriot rifleman, for instance, reportedly perched himself on a distant fence according to James Case's 1927 account, and fired thirty-two solo rounds at the retreating British column outside of Danbury without effect; nor was he hit when redcoat skirmishers returned fire.[9] Only by massing musket fire in controlled volleys could armies of the day inflict real damage on one another. And only through disciplined drill could a regiment be brought into play, company by company to administer such volleys.

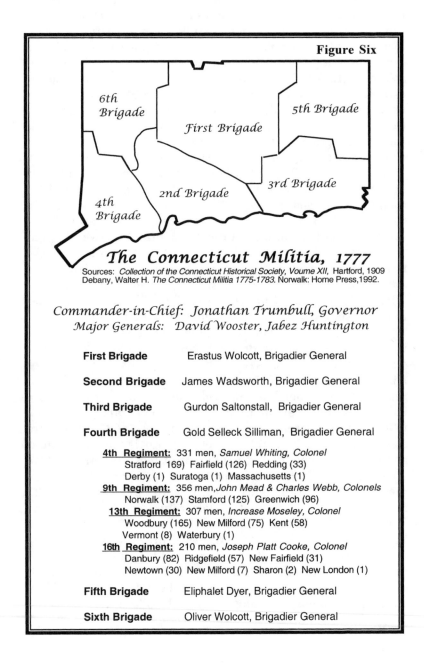

Figure Six

The Connecticut Militia, 1777

Sources: *Collection of the Connecticut Historical Society, Voume XII,* Hartford, 1909
Debany, Walter H. *The Connecticut Militia 1775-1783.* Norwalk: Home Press,1992.

Commander-in-Chief: Jonathan Trumbull, Governor
Major Generals: David Wooster, Jabez Huntington

First Brigade   Erastus Wolcott, Brigadier General

Second Brigade   James Wadsworth, Brigadier General

Third Brigade   Gurdon Saltonstall, Brigadier General

Fourth Brigade   Gold Selleck Silliman, Brigadier General

> **4th Regiment:** 331 men, *Samuel Whiting, Colonel*
> Stratford 169) Fairfield (126) Redding (33)
> Derby (1) Suratoga (1) Massachusetts (1)
> **9th Regiment:** 356 men,*John Mead & Charles Webb, Colonels*
> Norwalk (137) Stamford (125) Greenwich (96)
> **13th Regiment:** 307 men, *Increase Moseley, Colonel*
> Woodbury (165) New Milford (75) Kent (58)
> Vermont (8) Waterbury (1)
> **16th Regiment:** 210 men, *Joseph Platt Cooke, Colonel*
> Danbury (82) Ridgefield (57) New Fairfield (31)
> Newtown (30) New Milford (7) Sharon (2) New London (1)

Fifth Brigade   Eliphalet Dyer, Brigadier General

Sixth Brigade   Oliver Wolcott, Brigadier General

Fairfield County's militia ranks were mostly filled with shopkeepers, tradesmen, farmers and farmboys who, while comfortable with firearms, had long since traded muskets for plowshares to put food on the table. Salem Massachusetts officer Timothy Pickering Americanized British drill manuals in his *Easy Plan of Discipline for a Militia* in early 1775, but due to shortage of powder throughout the United Colonies most Fairfield men had little training in regimental field tactics or mass-volley discharge. Simply firing a musket in unison, for example, required twelve distinct motions and at least nine separate commands:

Command	Task
"Handle Cartridge"	Remove a cartridge from the belt box
"Tear Cartridge"	Grip cartridge in teeth & tear open
"Prime"	Pour powder from cartridge into chamber
"Close Frizzen"	Flip metal plate over the chamber
"Load"	Insert shot into barrel of gun
"Ram"	Use rod to ram shot home
"Full Cock"	With right thumb, cock the hammer
"Present"	Level the weapon at a target
"Fire"	Pull trigger

On parade grounds this manual of arms was tough enough to perform together; in rough terrain with one eye on gleaming bayonets of the approaching redcoat professionals, it was nearly impossible. Because militia units were armed with a bewildering variety of muskets, carbines and fowling pieces of varying lengths and caliber, cartridges (ball and shot packed in stiff paper) might be too large for one weapon and too small for another. Even worse, a musket was liable to be put out of action in wet weather when the cartridge powder became damp. To prevent such calamity, militiamen resorted to special individual pouches or hollowed-out cow horns to keep their powder dry. For all these reasons, hurriedly-formed irregulars like Wooster's command could barely deliver an organized volley, much less stand up to bayonets.

Even the more experienced Continental Army units were slow to develop confidence or discipline to engage British regulars head-on. In capturing Long Island and New York, Howe's professionals demonstrated their superior martial skills by intentionally absorbing an initial Patriot volley, then attacking quickstep fashion to disembowel their enemy with bayonet before repeat volleys could be organized. (George Washington was reportedly reduced to tears watching several regiments skewered in this fashion at Brooklyn Heights.) Consequently Patriot soldiers, particularly raw militia, tended to fall back into the protection of trees after discharging their first rounds, or even worse, take flight. To counter this collective instinct for self-preservation, officers (who had not become unaccountably ill) were forced to position themselves openly in front of the enemy and exhort their charges to follow. As a result, Patriot militia officer casualty rates often exceeded their British counterparts.

By flinging himself back in harm's way on the road to Ridgefield, then, David Wooster was simply doing what was expected of any senior militia officer. Securing a second mount, he rode boldly into the field of fire to rally his timid men, shouting something to the effect: *"Come on my boys, never mind such random shots! Follow me."* [10] Instantly, a musket ball ploughed through Wooster's waist, severing the spinal cord and knocking him from his horse.

> *Wooster's fatal shot is said to have been fired by an American Loyalist who carried a musket of unusual length, from a barn east of the road and on the right of the British rearguard as it appeared after facing about. Recognizing General Wooster, although the latter was almost three hundred yards away, the Tory asked permission to fire at the American general. 'You shall not do so,' replied the officer. 'The distance is too great for the shot and the attempt will subject us to retaliation.' Persisting in his request, the Tory caused his officer to finally yield and he fired with remarkable accuracy.* [11]

Other accounts suggest the range was much closer, a more likely event since most muskets of the period were virtually impossible to control with accuracy beyond fifty or sixty yards. One Colonel Hanger who served in America with Tarleton's Loyalist Legion had this to say: **"and as to firing at a man at 200 yards with a common musket, you may as well fire at the moon...."**[12] Whatever the distance, Wooster collapsed immediately from the ball that lodged in his back. His large sash unwound to serve as a makeshift stretcher, the fallen general was carried to the rear and laid on a large flat rock along the westerly side of the road, where his wound was dressed by a military doctor named Turner. Paralyzed, Wooster was then transported by carriage to Danbury and ultimately tended by Silliman's 4th Brigade departmental physician, Dr. Isaac Foster, in the very building that General Tyron had personally occupied the previous night — Tory Nehemiah Dibble's home.

But David Wooster was not alone earlier as he lay paralyzed on a wayside outcropping. Wounded about the same time, and attended to on the very same rock, was Major Thaddeus Crane of nearby North Salem, New York. Shot through the body, boots full with blood as he slipped off his mount, Crane was to survive another quarter-century until his passing in September of 1803. Also treated for wounds was Sergeant Daniel Bull of the 16th militia regiment, while Joel Hinman of Woodbury received a British ball in the upper left thigh that he carried another thirty-three years until finally extracted in 1810.

Confused and disorganized after Wooster's demise, the retreating Patriot militia subsequently scattered for cover. Joseph Jessup and Thaddeus Sterling of Wilton Parish, along with Sergeant James Lockwood of the 4th Westchester Militia, claimed in their pension requests to have been nearby when Wooster fell, but none chose to elaborate on what ensued; high tailing it into the woods, after all, was not likely to impress many pension examiners. John Eells from Stamford's Canaan Parish, who also saw Wooster fall, was more forthcoming...at least with his namesake son. Seeking a pension for his widowed mother, Eells Jr. later repeated his father's tale:

> I have often heard my father tell the story of that battle, ... and Father, having just discharged his musket, thought it not best to retreat with an empty gun. He loaded his musket and was just on the start when the belt of his cartridge belt broke and spilled out all his cartridges. He stooped down and picked them up and when he rose up he found himself far behind his comrades and but a few rods in advance of the British Army. He ran a short distance and the balls flew so thick that he stopped for a minute behind a large chestnut tree in hopes that the shower would abate. As there seemed

to be no cessation of the firing, he again retreated with all possible speed and finally creaped [*sic*] away without injury....[13]

Like Eells, most of Wooster's fleeing command found shelter among the surrounding trees. But even this safety proved elusive for the area was pocked with parties of camp followers and Loyalist light horse that had attached themselves to Tryon's force as early as the previous morning. In the confusion, Loyalists and Patriot militia intermingled in a myriad of harrowing undergrowth encounters. Several years later, A. B. Hull recorded *his* father's (then a seventeen-year-old Danbury militiaman) frightening experience:

> *In escaping one of the dashes of the enemy, he found himself back of a rock, in company with two boys a trifle younger than himself, who were having their first experience in battle. While waiting there he discovered that a Tory was in a brake nearby, watching with ready gun for them to reappear. Putting his hat on the end of a gun, he pushed it out beyond the rock. Immediately the Tory fired, the bullet piercing the hat. The next instant he plunged toward the rock, when the three boys fired simultaneously at him. At the discharge he sprang several feet into the air and came down full length upon his face, but turned in a flash upon his back, and lay there, motionless, in death.*[14]

"The panic of the rebel troops is confined and of short duration; the enthusiasm is extensive and permanent," observed General John Burgoyne in a brief to Lord Germain after his unexpected defeat at Saratoga.[15] Burgoyne may as well have been describing Wooster's men, for his aide, Captain Stephen R. Bradley, soon consolidated the scattered Patriot militia. A native of Cheshire Connecticut, the twenty-three-year-old Bradley (Yale 1775) must have been charismatic beyond his years, for he not only rallied Wooster's troops, but also rose later to the rank of general and became one of Vermont's very first United States senators.

Wooster's small command formally devolved to 16th Militia Colonel Joseph Platt Cooke of Danbury, who having finally arrived on the scene was the most senior officer present.[16] Most accounts agree that Bradley (or Cooke) then *attempted* to march to Ridgefield in advance of the British, and join Arnold and Silliman at the barricade, but no such arrival is mentioned in either general's formal report, or in pension applications of the two aforementioned Wilton men who saw Wooster fall. Since the addition of several hundred additional men at the barricade could hardly go unrecorded, it's safe to assume that Bradley and Cooke's force remained in the woods on Tryon's rear or flank.

Although no British casualties can be assigned with certainty to Wooster's second engagement, indeed British accounts dismissed the action as a mere "harassment," the affair occupied the rearguard field pieces long enough to briefly delay Tryon's progress, thereby giving Arnold and Silliman more precious time to fortify their defensive position a mile-and-a-half down the road in Ridgefield.

V. Decision at the Barricade

The Patriot command trio chose well when selecting Ridgefield to intercept Tryon's column, for more than two centuries later the position's natural defensive advantages are still quite discernable. After marching half a mile up-hill along North Salem Road, the British regiments would have to squeeze through a knoll-top notch situated at the northern end of Ridgefield's central ridge. Here a barricade of timbers, wagons and carts, stones and earth, anything the little Connecticut army could gather in one short hour for that purpose, was hastily erected astride the main road.

To the right, a sixty-year-old farmhouse extended the barricade perhaps another thirty yards, after which a pronounced slope fell off to marshy swamp. Still on file at Ridgefield town hall is a nineteenth-century map[1] that details a network of fieldstone farmyard walls further extending the defensive perimeter. The old map (*Figure Seven,* page 65) also reveals a small stream, referred to as "Steep Brook" in town land records, curling southward at the slope's base to protect the American right flank. A daunting series of no-longer-existing ledges loomed over more marshland on the barricade's left. This rocky promontory was free of any buildings during the Revolution, although Abner Gilbert blasted away the stone twenty years later to create space for his grand residence. Providing an avenue of escape to the American rear, Town Street stretched more than a mile through the village itself, then wound its way downhill toward Wilton Parish. Here, on this protected ridge with its secure exit, Arnold and Silliman could take on a larger force and retire gracefully.

Revisiting battlefield geography is vastly easier than reconstructing the action itself. No master list of individuals or units survives to tell us exactly who fought at Ridgefield, nor do General Arnold and General Silliman's formal reports provide any real detail about troop deployment. All we know for certain (from Silliman) is that bodies of militia were assigned to each wing, while the remaining troops (estimated at 200 by the April 30, 1777 *Connecticut Journal*) manned the barricade blocking Town Street's northern extremity. The sole surviving official troop summary document is a simple two-page list of individual reimbursement requests for hospital expenses, company and regimental payrolls, and other services rendered over the four-day Danbury Alarm. This "Record of Militia Service, 1777, The Danbury Raid"[2] contains 174 names, but fails to specify regiment affiliations, much less dates and places each man fought.

Like scattered ashes of a long-dead campfire, the real story of April 27, 1777 lay buried in dozens of individual participant records strewn across the state; only by tracking down each soldier, one by one, town by town, could the day's bloody work be recaptured. Personal diaries and correspondence, veterans' pension applications, musty turn-of-the-century town histories, obscure state archival documents, self-published family genealogies, and oral tradition yielded different pieces of the historical puzzle. Altogether, I was able to place 135 Americans with certainty at Ridgefield, while unearthing a nugget or two about seventy-nine individual contributions. Fitted together, these human puzzle pieces reveal a compelling picture of the short but brutal collision constituting the third and chief engagement at the barricade.

Although what follows may sometimes read like a historical novel, it most assuredly is not! Every name and action is fully documented (See Appendix B). Still, all seventy-nine individual stories did not take place simultaneously, and it fell to the author to restring them like so many pearls in a broken necklace. Because even eyewitness accounts might disagree in matters of sequence — especially when under enemy fire — a pearl or two are undoubtedly out of place. The thread (my narrative) may be new, but the necklace itself is quite authentic.

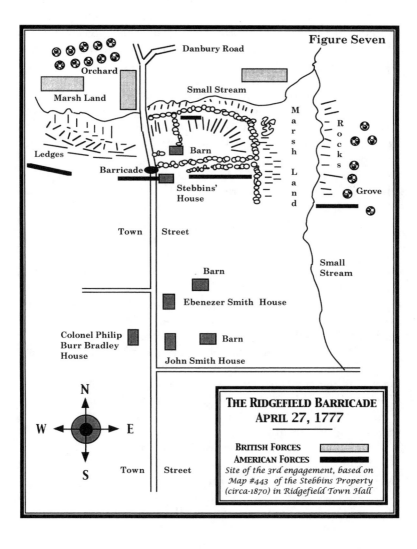

Figure Seven

THE RIDGEFIELD BARRICADE
APRIL 27, 1777

BRITISH FORCES
AMERICAN FORCES

Site of the 3rd engagement, based on Map #443 of the Stebbins Property (circa-1870) in Ridgefield Town Hall

First on the Scene

About six o'clock Sunday morning, Arnold and Silliman broke camp at Bethel Parish and stationed their troops at a near-by crossroad until Tryon's intentions could be determined. By nine it was clear the British were headed for Ridgefield via Ridgebury and Arnold put his force in motion through West Redding, traversed present-day Haviland Road at the Ridgefield border, then veered south along Danbury Road. Five-hundred-strong,[3] they arrived in Ridgefield two hours later. While Arnold's youthful dash (he was only 36) and sparkling combat reputation undoubtedly attracted farmers to his side en route, the bulk of his command consisted of Gold Selleck Silliman's 4th Brigade of Connecticut militia.

On paper the 4th Brigade's four regiments could boast more than 1,200 men; in reality little more than a third had answered Silliman's alarm two days earlier. Despite the presence of a formidable British Army in their own backyard — or more likely because of it — in truth most Fairfield militiamen stayed home. Colonel Hugh Hughes, a quartermaster of General Gates' Northern Army who arrived on the Ridgefield scene shortly after the engagement, disappointedly observed: **"I believe the whole of our force did not exceed 4 or 5 hundred, so amazingly slow did the inhabitants turn out on this alarming occasion."** [4]

Twenty-two-year-old Nehemiah Banks of Fairfield is a prime example. Banks had previously served three separate terms as a private during '75 & '76 under Silliman in New York. He participated in the costly defense of Fort Washington during the Patriot withdrawal from New York and would go on to participate in the victory at Saratoga in the fall of 1777, be taken prisoner in Rhode Island the following year and, when exchanged, serve in the field during both the 1779 and 1780 campaigns. Clearly Banks knew what he was about, yet his pension application shows Nehemiah chose not to answer Silliman's call on April 25, 1777.[5] Woefully short of experienced men like Banks, Silliman's Fairfield County militia was little more than "Raw levies, chiefly old men and boys."[6]

Still, most of southwestern Connecticut was represented in Silliman's 4th Brigade ranks: Colonel Samuel Whiting's 4th Regiment from Fairfield, Stratford, and Redding; the 9th Regiment from Norwalk, Stamford, and Greenwich (Colonel John Mead); and the 13th Regiment from Woodbury, New Milford, Kent (Colonels Benjamin Hinman and Increase Mosely). Silliman's remaining regiment was the 16th Militia from Danbury, Ridgefield, Newtown and New Fairfield (Colonel Joseph Platt Cooke), whom we met earlier and now lay on Tryon's rear as part of the unfortunate General Wooster's dispersed command.

Fairfield County's 4th Militia Brigade was welcomed to Ridgefield by a newly formed contingent of raw local irregulars known as the 1st Ridgefield Militia under Captain Ebenezer Jones, whose farmhouse (today's Brewster Farm) lay about a mile and a half to the east of Town Street. Depleted by sixteen men released earlier in the week to Continental service, Jones' command included no more than a few dozen farmers and shopkeepers such as cabinet-maker Elisha Hawley. Grandson of the town's original minister, Hawley was a Congregational Church deacon, perhaps the choir's finest voice, and the only Ridgefield Revolutionary War veteran who went on to serve in the War of 1812. Among Hawley's militia companions were Seth Bouton, Stephen Olmstead, Elijah Smith, Abel Pulling, and Michael Warren.

Also at Arnold's disposal was a cadre from the newly reconstituted 5th Connecticut Regiment of the Continental Line. In the throes of reorganization, much of the 5th Regiment was en route to, or encamped at, Peekskill New York, as directed on April 14th by Commander-in-Chief of the Connecticut Line, General Samuel Parsons. Regimental Colonel Philip Burr Bradley, however, was at his Ridgefield home this day, for two months earlier General Washington requested Connecticut Governor Trumbull inoculate new levies for smallpox before releasing them to Continental service, and Bradley had advised Washington in late March that he was **"appointed by General Parsons to superintend the smallpox in the western end of this state."**[7] With Colonel Bradley, presumably awaiting inoculation or freshly released from quarantine, was an undetermined number of the forty-three locals who had enlisted in the 5th Connecticut before April 27.[8]

Bradley's men may even have sported portions of their brown (yes, brown) uniforms for the very first time because **"171 felt hats, the same number of men's shoes and the same number of stockings"** were directed to the unit by the state on April 4th.[9] After consulting with General Washington in 1775 the Continental Congress mandated brown, not blue, as official color for American military uniforms. In fact, most Connecticut troops, as vividly documented by the writings and watercolors of Revolutionary War historian Charles Macklin Lefferts (1873-1923), remained brown-clad until General Washington prescribed blue for all branches of the army in his directive of October 2, 1779. One highly noticeable exception was Colonel Jedediah Huntington's 1st Connecticut Regiment of the Continental Line that, like Colonel Webb's 4th Connecticut, sported bright red tunics taken from British supply vessels captured on the high seas by privateers. Another likely exception was Colonel Bradley himself, for most senior American officers chose to wear blue from the onset.

However clad, the 5th Connecticut contingent included Lieutenant Benjamin Smith (a Town Street resident), brown-complexioned black-haired Sergeant Clement Lloyd (who was to die next day at Compo), Private David Coggin, and Ebenezer Patchen of Redding, whose brother Jacob had been taken prisoner by Tryon the day before. Ridgefield brothers Bradley and Jeremiah Dean had enlisted in the 5th only four days earlier and were likely awaiting their smallpox vaccinations. Bradley Dean may well have landed a position as fifer in the regimental color guard since he had previously served in that capacity with the 4th Connecticut Militia. Another fresh recruit was the black slave, Jack Congo.

Black soldiers were not unusual in New England's Continental regiments, for slave owners often "enlisted" their charges and received the soldiers' monthly pay. One Dover Davison, for example, joined Bradley's regiment in 1777 and, upon his death three years later, Norwalk owner Stephen St. John petitioned Bradley for back pay.[10] Enlisting in the Fifth Connecticut a month before the Ridgefield fray, Jack Congo was a black servant of Nathaniel Baldwin. Congo survived the action in Ridgefield, but perished the following year, whereupon Baldwin, of course, subsequently solicited Colonel Bradley for any wages due.[11]

A Ridgefield resident since matriculating from Yale in 1758, forty-one-year-old Colonel Philip Burr Bradley clearly participated in the upcoming engagement, as evidenced by a bill for his services submitted to the state comptroller's office. Bradley's large gambrel-colonial Main Street residence was, in fact, no more than 150 yards south of Arnold's barricade! It appears, however, that the good colonel contributed much more than "services rendered" to the defense of Ridgefield, as evidenced by Bradley's subsequent £30 reimbursement petition to the General Assembly:

> As the enemy retreated thru [*sic*] the town of Ridgefield near the Memorialist's dwelling house, said Memorialist was obliged and actually did deliver out of his own property about one hundred and twenty gallons of Rum for the refreshment of the troops.[12]

A ration of rum prior to battle was not uncommon for Revolutionary soldiers on both sides. Time-permitting, a commanding officer might energize his charges by dispensing a four-ounce dose, known as a "gill." Special celebration might even justify half a pint, but Bradley's 120 gallons translates to nearly a quart of rum for every man present! Astute politician and experienced soldier, Bradley undoubtedly knew Tryon's British regulars would ultimately overrun the Patriot barricade and confiscate any large trove of Yankee spirits. Rather than see his regimental rum slake enemy thirsts, the Colonel most likely distributed his stores generously to all at hand. It would seem, then, that the "Spirit of '76" was significantly fortified by spirits of another kind among those who stared down at the approaching British army. Or, was the good colonel simply padding his expenses?

Given General Arnold's well-known mistrust of militia, it's safe to assume the Patriot center was anchored by the 5th Connecticut. Bradley's men may not have been the only Continentals to man Arnold's makeshift breastworks, since Rockwell noted that Captain Samuel Lawrence's company of Westchester regulars was also at hand. However, Rockwell may have mistaken the New Yorkers' affiliation because formal state returns list Samuel Lawrence as captain of militia (3rd Westchester Regiment).[13] In addition to Lawrence's teenage son, the Salem contingent included one Squire Holmes of Boutonville, New York (a flag-bearer according to Bedini), Moses Bouton, Abraham Smith, Sergeant Lebbeus Mead, and fifteen-year-old Stamfordite David Selleck, whose father had been captured the previous fall during the battle for Long Island and would die in British captivity. Young David was visiting the Salem home of his uncle Gershom Selleck, when "in spite of his mother's entreaties, he shouldered a musket and hurried to the fight."[14]

Somewhere along the barricade, Captain Jones and Lieutenant Joseph Darling positioned the 1st Ridgefield militia. They were joined by local farmers such as 50-year-old Dublin-born Robert Edmond from the Florida District and his son William, a senior at Yale College. Wealthy Upper Salem farmer Timothy Delavan also made an appearance, arriving on horseback with his nine armed sons in tow. Sixteen-year-old Jeremiah Keeler, younger brother of tavern-owner Timothy Keeler Jr., had already served two three-month stints in the 9th Militia regiment, and having displayed military aptitude since age fourteen, joined his fellow townsmen near the barricade. Also nearby was Captain David Olmstead, whose little one-and-a-half story "saltbox" home still stands in the south end of town along (what else) but Olmstead Lane. Olmstead, it may be recalled, was one of the first Ridgefield men to commit to the Patriot cause, having led a company to Washington's army in early '76. The Commander-in-Chief must have made a forceful impression on the twenty-seven-year-old captain, for on this very day one year earlier (April 27, 1776), he named a newly born son "George Washington" Olmstead! In addition to defending his home and four young children, Captain Olmstead had scores to settle with the redcoats — cousin Roger fell in action in 1775, and cousin David was killed January 4th, 1777 in Washington's victory at Princeton.

Arnold Deploys his Militia

Reminiscing about his wartime experiences some seventy years later, Jeremiah Keeler recalled that the American flanks extended to two roads **"about eighty rods east and west from Ridgefield Street and parallel with it."**[15] Along these two roads, today known as High Ridge and Grove Streets, General Arnold secured both flanks with Silliman's southwestern Connecticut militia. The right flank, to the east of the barricade at the head of present day Grove Street, was manned by soldier-farmers of the 4th Militia Regiment, who trained their muskets on the marshy stream that any British flanking party would have to cross. Led by Colonel Samuel Whiting and seconded by Lieutenant Colonel Abraham Gould, the 4th Regiment was composed primarily of Fairfield and Stratford men.

Ebenezer Coe and William Thompson had been among the first Stratford men to openly embrace the Patriot cause; both men were named to Stratford's Committee of Inspection to smoke out flagrant Tories two years before, and both were commissioned as militia officers in 1776. Coe had even been taken prisoner in the battle for Long Island, but the enterprising Yankee escaped unharmed. This day the twosome commanded Stratford Companies of the 4th Militia Regiment, Coe as a full captain, and Lieutenant Thompson in place of his captain who was detained at home by a "peculiar sickness" that often visited timid officers. Perhaps the pair joked together about the absent captain's malady while positioning their men on the American right flank.

A similar-sized militia force occupied High Ridge Road on the left wing — undoubtedly the 13th Regiment commanded by Colonels Benjamin Hinman and Increase Mosely of Woodbury. Staunchly patriotic, Woodbury fielded eight militia companies in 1777, at least three of which were at Ridgefield under captains Leavenworth, Judson and Hinman (one of twenty-eight to serve from this family during the Revolution). Among their charges were Privates Thomas Torrance, Justus Johnson, and Simeon and Timothy Mather.

His brigade deployed, General Silliman remained with Arnold in the center accompanied by Lieutenant Colonel David Dimon of the 6th Connecticut Line, a socially prominent

Fairfield friend. One of the first Connecticut men responding
to Massachusetts' call in the wake of Lexington and Concord,
Dimon had acted with equal alacrity in putting the Fairfield
militia in motion upon Tryon's arrival. Thomas Dimon, taken
prisoner outside Fairfield, was somewhere in the British
column, and three other Dimons were in Silliman's militia
command. As the eldest, Colonel Dimon was surely keeping a
watchful eye over his kinsmen and hoping for an opportunity
to free the captured Thomas.

Barricade defended and flanks protected, General
Arnold then placed skirmishers in front of his line to engage
the approaching British. Between 1844 and 1850, John D.
McDonald interviewed 241 people aged seventy to ninety-six
as fieldwork for his 1,001-page manuscript detailing
Westchester County's role in the Revolution. One participant,
eighty-nine-year-old Thaddeus Bell of Middlesex Parish
(Darien), vividly recalled his experience of seventy years
earlier, when he found himself in the skirmishing party
Arnold had positioned between the Patriot breastworks and
oncoming British column:

> ...I belonged to Capt. Jesse Bell's Coast Guards and
> marched to Ridgefield, where on the ___ of April we
> were posted north of Stebbins' house where the road
> turned to go to Danbury.... We were posted to take the
> British in the flank as they came down the Ridgebury
> Road. We were behind the fence and eight to ten rods
> north of Stebbins' barn.... The British advanced with
> music which we heard along [sic] time before they
> reached us. When they saw us they fired, but fired
> too high.[16]

Loosely attached to Colonel Mead's 9th Militia
Regiment, Captain Jesse Bell's company usually had the job
of protecting the Stamford and Middlesex Parish (Darien)
coast from Loyalist raids. These "Coast Guards" were
accomplished sailors who had previously distinguished
themselves in hand-to-hand combat during small craft actions
on Long Island sound. Before the engagement heated up,
however, Bell's skirmishers would have retreated to the
Stebbins barn (*Figure Seven*), then back to the main Patriot
position.

Waiting behind the barricade was a second Stamford company of Mead's 9th Militia Regiment whose ranks included John Holmes, David Stevens, David Waterbury, and Benjamin Weed, Samuel Waterbury, Nathaniel and Thaddeus Husted, Annanias, Jabez and Smith Weed, and Eleazar Hoyt. A third Stamford company about forty strong from Canaan Parish was led by the very deaf Captain John Carter and seconded by Lieutenant Hezekiah Davenport of lower Ponus Ridge Road. Colonel Mead himself would have been easy to spot, for he was a short, fleshy man whose vest, a tailor is said to have jokingly observed, would wrap around five men.

The rotund Mead had commanded a company in King's service before the Revolution and refused a regular army Crown commission at War's onset, persevering in service of the Revolutionary cause for the conflict's full duration. Mead's patriotism exacted a stiff price, for only months before Tryon's raid, Loyalist "cowboys" repeatedly plundered his Greenwich backcountry home until it was torn to pieces and emptied of livestock and crops.

Alongside the Stamford men stood a Norwalk militia company captained by Ozias Marvin. Father of eight and town selectman, the 40-year-old Marvin was a prosperous Norwalk tavern owner/carpenter who had rallied his company the day before in response to the Danbury alarm. Failing to mobilize in time to help Silliman's Fairfield militia chase down Tryon's column, Marvin then bivouacked his little command along the Saugatuck River together with a company of Stamford militia. As the men huddled outdoors that blustery, wet night, Ozias Marvin claimed to have generously distributed forty-five gallons of rum and sixty pounds of dried beef from his own tavern larder. Receiving word of Tryon's location on Sunday morning, the Norwalk and Stamford contingents then marched directly to Ridgefield.

From New Milford came John Terrill, William Noble, William Drinkwater, David Buell and Reuben Phillips. Captain Azor Belden, a veteran of Bunker Hill, led a Wilton cohort in which only Lieutenant Matthew Gregory and Theophilius Mead can be placed with certainty. Meanwhile physician Levi Ives and noted apothecary Dr. David Atwater, having most likely accompanied Arnold and Wooster from New Haven the night before, set up shop in the Stebbins

House for the grim business that lay ahead. Joining them was young Surgeon's Mate Amos Baker, a Ridgefield native who would two years later marry Stebbins' granddaughter, Sarah, establish a surgeon's practice in town, and erect his household no more than sixty yards from Arnold's breastworks.

Possibly somewhere in the Patriot ranks with Colonel Mosely, but most likely still on the march after receiving the midnight alarm, was a company of Litchfield militia, armed with fifty of the most storied bullets in the Rebel arsenal. Amidst local hysteria following Congress's long-awaited Declaration of Independence the previous July, a spirited contingent of Connecticut militia helped topple a huge gilt lead equestrian statue of King George III from its pedestal on the bowling green at Broadway's lower end near the Battery. This prize was secreted away to Litchfield (although the equine head purportedly materialized in Wilton Parish), where General Oliver Wolcott had it chopped up and melted down to make 42,088 precious lead musket balls, fifty of which were doled out to the local militia.

Could the Patriots also have had artillery support at Ridgefield? The previous day in Redding, according to James Case's 1927 account, General Silliman's militia brigade was accompanied by *"parts of the companies of Colonel Lamb's battalion of artillery with three rusty cannon, a field piece and part of the artillery company of Fairfield."* Congress had indeed created four artillery regiments of the Continental Line in January 1777, the second of which was commanded by Colonel John Lamb. The solons, however, neglected to provide any funding, so Benedict Arnold supplied £1000 from his own pocket to help equip his friend Lamb's new unit. Although largely from New York, the 2nd Regiment did include 170 Connecticut men, at least one company of which hailed from New Haven.

Revolutionary firebrand and early New York Sons of Liberty ringleader, John Lamb had forfeited his home and property when Howe's redcoats invested Manhattan Island. As a freshly commissioned New York artillery captain, Lamb met Benedict Arnold during the 1775 winter siege of Quebec, and the two kindred spirits became real friends. Lamb was captured in Arnold's failed New Year's Eve assault on

Quebec's ramparts and, face horribly disfigured by grapeshot, spent six painful months in a British prison. After being exchanged (and promoted), Lamb then removed with his family to Southington, Connecticut. Informed that the New Haven battery of his command had followed Arnold to Danbury, Lamb mounted-up and galloped hell-for-leather to the scene.

Did Lamb or his guns arrive in time? The artillery did not. Although a battery would have put real teeth in Ridgefield's primitive breastworks, the fieldpieces mentioned by Case (and the *Connecticut Journal* of April 30, 1777) were too slow and unwieldy to accompany Arnold and Silliman's rapid cross-country maneuver across muddy West Redding earlier that rainy morning. In fact, no formal report or individual participant account from either side mentions American cannon until next day at Saugatuck. As for Lamb, the hard-riding colonel apparently reached Ridgefield as the battle waned, but in the prevailing confusion his small party was unable to connect with the American command.[17] Isaac Leake's 1857 *Life of Lamb* tells us it was not until the following afternoon (Monday, April 28th) that he finally caught up with Arnold at Saugatuck Bridge — whereupon the valiant Colonel Lamb was wounded severely enough to be listed as "killed" in British returns.

Tryon Reaches the Barricade

Spiraling clouds of black smoke striated the sky over smoldering Danbury ten miles to the north, while a fresher plume from Isaac Keeler's gristmill provided telltale evidence that Tryon's column was headed this way. Of course the men behind Ridgefield's barricade could not have known that only a fraction of Danbury's dwellings had been put to the torch, and must have imagined a much worse fate — one they might soon share. Soon the crackle of Wooster's musket fire and the boom of more disciplined British volleys could be heard in the distance, punctuated by an occasional artillery blast.

Loyalist Epenetus How(e)'s fine circa-1750 clapboard, center-chimney, post-and-beam framed house was perched on the west side of North Salem Road a half mile below the

American ridge-top breastworks. As the British column filed past How(e)'s doorstep:

> *It was reported that a spy was secreted in this house and when soldiers tried to enter they found it barricaded. One tried to get in by window and received several cuts on his fingers from a butcher knife used by an inmate of the house. Marks remained on the windowsill for many years.*[18]

Observed by historian George Rockwell in 1927, the knife marks are indisputable, but a direct descendant of How(e) claimed they resulted from an earlier Patriot attempt to intrude while the How(e)s were at dinner. The presence of a Patriot spy under the roof of a known Loyalist *does* seem quite improbable; more likely Tryon's officers sensed that action loomed ahead and simply searched the house to flush out any potential snipers in their rear. Indeed, another story told in the How(e) family relates that:

> *British officers entered the house and searched it. Howe was the father of twin infant daughters, named Nancy and Betsey. An officer picked one of them out of the cradle, and holding the infant aloft said 'If you are Tories, God Bless you! If you are not, God d- - n you!*[19]

We'll never know for certain which, if any, of these stories are true, but Ridgefield vital records indeed verify that twin daughters, Nancy and Elizabeth were born to the How(e)s nine months before on July 25, 1776. It's also worth noting that "two fine Revolutionary War muskets" were found in the attic when the house changed hands in 1922.[20]

How(e)'s house in their wake, Tryon's soldiers proceeded over the bridge spanning Titicus River, filed past the little red Titicus District schoolhouse on their right and Old Town Cemetery to their left, then faced Arnold's barricade. After driving off Captain Jesse Bell's skirmishers from behind stone walls to their left, the redcoat army came to a halt.

Fife and drum corps blaring and regimental colors flapping, the British army, according to General Silliman's formal report, **"appeared in One grand column that filled the Road for more than half a mile in length."** But the whole magnificent show fizzled to a standstill when Tryon, Erskine and Agnew paused to size up the situation ahead.

Up to this point Tryon's lightly contested march had been little more than a military parade. True there were a few casualties, but even Wooster's sacrifice was no more than a rear-guard harassment. Looming ahead, though, was promise of real action. The well-placed Patriot barricade commanded high ground and was protected by steep rocky ledges on its right flank. Any assault to the left would have to cross a small marshy creek, then, like Bunker (Breed's) Hill in miniature, ascend a slope laced with stonewalls. As the enemy skirmish line withdrew, no experienced military eye could have failed to notice the bristling muskets massed behind the makeshift Rebel breastwork, or the fluttering flag hinting at the presence of Continentals. And Benedict Arnold was regarded throughout His Majesty's army as an opponent who knew how to fight. Yes, any experienced officer could see the parade was over; men would die here.

But Tryon was no experienced officer. His only prior field command came six years earlier in North Carolina, when his militia prevailed over a backcountry mob in an action that was little more than the spontaneous collision of two lines. As for his stint in the Royal Foot Guards, all Tryon had to show (besides the handsome uniform) was an ignominious amphibious affair off the French coast in 1758 in which he nearly drowned as his regiment retreated by boat to offshore Royal Navy transports.[21]

Ambitious and vain as he may have been, William Tryon was no fool. Recognizing affairs were militarily over his head at Arnold's barricade, Tryon (if he had not already done so) then had the good sense to place tactical command in the capable hands of Sir William Erskine — an act not unnoticed by propagandistic Rebels. Seizing upon Tryon's discretion as cowardice, one Patriot wag ginned-up the sarcastic verse "Expedition to Danbury." Within a month, newspapers from Pennsylvania to South Carolina gleefully caricatured Tryon spouting this little ditty to his soldiers:

> In cunning and canting, deceit and disguise
> In cheating a friend, and inventing of lies,
> I think I'm a match for the best of my species,

But in this undertaking, I feel all in pieces;
So I'll fall to the rear, for I'd rather go last;-
Come, march on, my boys, let me see you all past;
For his Majesty's service (so says my commission)
Requires that I *bring up* the whole expedition.[22]

The Assault Begins

Having charged into the mouth of French cannons at
Fontenoy with one of the Empire's finest cavalry units (Scot's
Greys), General Sir William "Woolly" Erskine was not the
stuff of silly verse.   The Rebels had not been intimidated by
Tryon's show of force complete with massed musicians and
colors, so they would now dance to the tune of hot lead and
cold steel.   Erskine first concentrated the six artillery pieces
and commenced shelling the American position — but
Arnold's men stood their ground.   Units were next detailed to
either flank, where Silliman noted **"they were received
warmly by our Posts."**   Having quickly taken the measure
of his opponent, Erskine then beefed up both flanking parties
and massed at least 600 men into a central column to storm
the Patriot barricade.   Three field pieces were deployed in
front to cover the final assault.

When confronting an opponent on open field, British
units, like most eighteenth-century European armies, fought
in a line three men deep, the front rank kneeling and each
rank locked together by placing the left foot inside the right
foot of the man in front of him.   During the Seven Years War,
redcoat commanders learned that two-deep lines were more
practical than three in North America given the rough
terrain, absence of cavalry, and loosely structured nature of
combat.   Since these conditions still prevailed fifteen years
later, His Majesty's lines remained two-deep during the
Revolution.   But British tactics manuals[23] recommended an
altogether different approach — attacking in column — when
assaulting a fortified position such as Arnold's.   The idea was
to deprive defenders of the advantage of picking off attackers
in line before they could close for bayonet work.   Instead, a
rapidly moving, concentrated column could overpower
entrenched opponents with sheer mass at point of contact —

especially under cover of artillery support. By hurling a 600-man column at the Patriot barricade, Erskine was simply executing standard military doctrine.

Staring down from their wooden breastworks at a professional army more than thrice their number steadily advancing through the swirling smoke with fixed bayonets, Arnold's men followed the example of Captain Lawrence's Salem Company... and held their fire.

> *With Lawrence was his young son, who when he saw the British approaching, raised his rifle to shoot prematurely. With a blow of his sword, Lawrence knocked the weapon down.*[24]

Anchoring the barricade to young Lawrence's right stood a saltbox farmhouse that belonged to none other than Benjamin Stebbins, the elderly British sympathizer who two years earlier had led Ridgefield's reaffirmation of allegiance to King George. Now, in a devious twist of fate, Stebbins' house was about to receive the full fury of British arms!

> *Eighty-six-year-old Benjamin Stebbins hid in a Bedroom in the east attic. Being farthest from the scene of fire, he thought this room would be the safest, but...a bullet passed through the room near his head and bore a jagged hole through the bedroom door. The house caught fire several times during the battle, and son Josiah managed to extinguish the flames.*[25]

No two accounts agree upon the precise time of Erskine's assault. Arnold noted the affair began about an hour after his eleven AM Ridgefield arrival, but Silliman reported three o'clock in his dispatch to Connecticut governor Trumbull, and British Engineering officer Archibald Robertson had it as two PM. Nor was there consensus on the action's duration. Although Benedict Arnold's formal report to General Alexander McDougall referred to the affair as a **"smart action which lasted about an hour,"** his estimate undoubtedly consolidated the artillery bombardment and flanking probes together with the final British thrust. Other accounts note the barricade was taken in about fifteen minutes. British engineering officer Archibald Robertson jotted in his diary simply that: **"We immediately (2 o'clock)**

attack'd the village and drove them off and took possession."

Sometime, then, between noon and three in the afternoon, General Agnew was given the honor of leading Erskine's British assault. Later singled out for conspicuous bravery by Agnew's major of brigade, Lesslie, Major Stewart of the 15th Foot (or so Bedini tells us) rushed to the American line with only ten or twelve men behind him. Erskine's entire column then surged forward, triggering a murderous fire sufficiently loud to be recorded eighteen miles distant in William Wheeler's diary at Black Rock Harbor in Fairfield.[26]

At least sixteen redcoats died near the barricade alone, while perhaps another twenty-five were wounded. British guns and bayonets evened the score, claiming Lieutenant Nathaniel Gray of Redding and Easton farmer Samuel Seeley, whose death left six young children to feed. Seven more children became fatherless when 9th Militia Lieutenant Hezekiah Davenport of Canaan Parish fell dead. Stamford paid a terrible toll, for in addition to Davenport, David Stevens was killed, and Captain Jesse Bell was wounded along with Privates John Waterbury Jr. and Jonathan Travis. Private Isaac Richards' pension request (ultimately denied) described a musket ball wound in the left leg, but Richards survived to become New Canaan's very first First Selectman in 1801. Another Stamford man, Benjamin Weed, received a musket ball that remained under his skin the rest of his life, while cousin Smith Weed was wounded by a shot that passed through both thighs!

"In the action with the enemy at Ridgefield on their return from Danbury, I was wounded by a ball in the hip,"[27] wrote Theophilius Mead of Wilton thirty years later in his veteran's pension application. Abraham Smith, whose father-in-law, Major Thaddeus Crane, was hit earlier with Wooster, fell wounded and later died in his North Salem home. Somewhere in the fray, Sergeant Thomas Parmalee of Washington, Connecticut was wounded by a musket shot in the right thigh, while Private Isaiah Bunce's denied pension request tells of a painful leg wound. Captain Sylvanus Knapp of Greenwich shared Parmalee's fate, but the unfortunate Private Noah Bartlett, from Colonel Samuel Wylly's 3rd Connecticut Regiment of the Continental Line, was killed.

(Just what Bartlett was doing in Ridgefield is a mystery since his regiment consisted mostly of Hartford men and no other members can be traced to the action.)

Yale undergraduate William Edmond went down with a serious thigh wound that Woodbury physician Joseph Perry considered permanently crippling. Had not his father removed William to the nearby family farm, he may well have been finished off by bayonet. Young Bradley Dean's fife would never twitter in regimental review, for the 5th Connecticut veteran of all of four days perished near the barricade. Fellow Ridgefield 5th Connecticut private Solomon Brown survived the carnage — only to die of starvation at Valley Forge the following winter. Salem Sergeant Lebbeus Mead was hit by a ball in the right hip and left as dead. Mead survived, but David Selleck, the youth who ignored his mother's plea to remain in Salem, died in action. Rockwell asserted that Dr. David Atwater also met his end in Ridgefield, but other more reliable sources show Atwater was killed the next day at Compo Hill.

The Patriot Right Flank Collapses

"I was then on the flank guards..." remembered John Dibble of Middlesex Parish in 1847, **"...and five out of twenty five of us got killed."**[28] Facing superior numbers, the Patriot right flank was smashed and withdrew to safety behind East Ridge, but at least one redcoat went down, according to William Wheeler's Fairfield diary (1740-1811). Wheeler offers a graphic glimpse of the action as experienced by David Patchen, his wife's great-uncle and locally renowned pigeon hunter:

> . . . he had seven shots, when he took as he said as good a sight as ever he did at pigeons – the last time at one that came around the corner of the house about 3 rods distance. He saw him drop, and then under cover of smoke of the whole volley which the British poured in upon them, retreated, and when that left him, skulked behind a rock where the balls struck spat! spat! spat! in the manner of hail. The place where they retreated was a cleared spot through an orchard – no cover – and there Col. Gould of Fairfield was shot.[29]

Rallying his 4th Regiment of Connecticut militia, the forty-four-year-old Abraham Gould slumped dead in his saddle about a quarter-mile from the barricade, near a road (presumably present day Grove Street) that paralleled Ridgefield's Town Street. British volleys raked Gould's unit, killing forty-one-year-old Lieutenant Ephraim Middlebrook of Stratford. His Stratford neighbor, Captain Ebenezer Coe, also crumpled to the ground, later recalling that he:

> . . . received a musket ball through my head, cutting off part of my right ear and carrying away my right eye. I fell as dead, lay a time, but recovered to my thoughts, after being inhumanly stabbed with a bayonet in my side and my right hand while I lay unfeelingly as dead.[30]

Coe miraculously survived, perhaps through the help of an enemy officer:

> *Tradition explains further that while Captain Coe lay on the field wounded, a British soldier was about to pierce him with a bayonet when a superior officer severely reprimanded him, took up Captain Coe, carried him to a house nearby, examined his commission which was in his pocket, expressed his sorrow at being unable to give him further aid and withdrew.*[31]

Thirty-five-year-old Lieutenant William Thompson of Fairfield, gallantly filling in for his "sick" captain, was not so fortunate. In Captain Coe's own words: **"He was wounded and while in that condition a British soldier stepped up and blew his brains out with his gun."**[32] Coe's Company was hit hard: Lieutenant DeForest was shot in the leg, while Lieutenants Stephen Wells and Ephraim Curtis were both wounded. Private William Curtis, another Stratford man, and likely Ephraim's kin, was knocked to the ground by a musket ball in the left thigh. Somehow the foursome avoided poor Thompson's fate and limped away to safety. Frightened for his life, sixteen-year-old Joseph Hyde of Greens Farm Parish fled for cover, returning home unharmed. Another boy, John Brooks Jr. of Stratford, would later confess:

"I once asked him [Captain Coe] how it was that so
many officers were killed and wounded — He said it
was because the privates run off just before they were
flanked by the British."[33]

British accounts claim that Colonel Samuel Whiting
was also wounded, so after Colonel Gould went down, the
shattered 4th Militia Regiment dispersed as the right flank
dissolved. Sergeant Samuel Gold, Privates Robert Hawley
and George Lennon, and nineteen-year-old Stephen Fairchild,
one of six brothers in American service, all managed to flee
with wounds of their own. Another Redding Hawley, William
by name according to Bedini, likely had the harrowing
experience of seeing his brother Stephen near the barricade,
for Stephen had accompanied Montfort Browne's Prince of
Wales American Volunteer unit after restoring a stolen mount
to British General Agnew the previous Friday.

Although suffering few casualties (only Colonel
Hinman, Privates Edmond, Johnson and Torrance were
wounded), the Patriot left flank fared no better. According to
Abner Gilbert, whose residence was raised on the site after
Revolution's end: **"The British completely outflanked
and encircled Arnold's left wing, crowded them closely
together and compelled them to retreat in confusion."**[34]
Possibly led by General James Agnew himself, a lead
company from the British 44th Regiment of Foot navigated a
fruit orchard, slogged through the marsh at the foot of
precipitous ledges, scaled the cliffs and with fixed bayonet
surprised the defenders to the barricade's left. Other reports
indicate that Agnew was in the center, and may have been
incapacitated by a minor head wound. Another source
claimed Agnew's wound was in the shoulder. Whoever its
leader, the 44th Foot then turned its attention to Arnold's
remaining troops in the center. Simultaneously Tryon's main
column reached the makeshift barricade itself.

Benedict Arnold's Heroics

Virtually every eyewitness and secondary source
confirms that at this point in the action Benedict Arnold

displayed extraordinary courage under fire, but few agree on the exact details.   One scenario, romanticized by oral tradition, has Arnold personally directing the evacuation of his men from the barricade, only to find himself exposed between the advancing enemy and his retreating soldiers. A second, more plausible version, based on McDonald's eyewitness interviews and Arnold's impetuous nature, suggests the future turncoat was leading a volunteer party *forward* to dislodge the redcoat vanguard of the 44th Foot who had just clambered over the ledges at the barricade's left. In either case, what happened next is beyond dispute, as reported three days later in the *Connecticut Journal*:

> The General had his horse shot under him, when the enemy were within about ten yards of him, but luckily received no hurt, recovering himself he drew his pistols and shot the soldier who was advancing with his fixed bayonet.[35]

Arnold may well have been fired upon by an entire platoon! Historian Benson Lossing visited Ridgefield in 1850 to research his *Pictorial History of the Revolution* and heard from an old man (perhaps Abner Gilbert) that: "*. . . on the day after the battle himself and some other boys skinned Arnold's horse and discovered nine bullet holes in his hide.*" [36] Lossing's tale may indeed have merit, for a 1925 Ridgefield Press article described the unearthing of skeletal equine remains at the precise location where Arnold's unfortunate mount was reputedly buried. (A rustic little hand-made wooden sign still clings to a tree on the west side of Town [Main] Street marking the spot near the barricade where Arnold's horse reportedly fell.)

Tradition has it that Arnold's bayonet-wielding attacker was no redcoat, but rather a Tory, and a dialogue ensued between the two:

> While struggling to release his feet from the stirrups, a Tory named Coon from New Fairfield or New Milford advanced, saying 'Surrender! You are my prisoner,' 'Not yet,' said Arnold who drew a pistol and shot the man dead.[37]

A century later, local Congregational Church minister and amateur historian Edward Teller had Arnold saying: "*one* to meet the needs of white students but forget the different needs of minorities.

5. *Change the use of standardized test scores.* Tests tend to engender strongly positive or strongly negative feelings among educators, and both sides of the argument have validity. Tests can provide objective, standardized information that is useful in evaluating schools or students, diagnosing scholastic or personality problems, and placing students in proper courses. However, tests are often abused—they are overinterpreted, they become ends in themselves, and, perhaps more importantly, they serve middle-class white students best.

If we were to eliminate all tests tomorrow, would racism go away? Would teachers have higher expectations for blacks? Would they stop trying to label those they think are smartest and not put this in their students' records? Hardly! This would only make our racism more subjective. Tests simply reflect the system, and if the system is racist, the tests are too.

The solution is to improve testing procedures and broaden the definition of tests to include quantifiable data. Developing tests and other measures (which may not be the paper-and-pencil type) is not only possible but practical. Our work on developing new admission predictors, culturally relevant intelligence tests, and the Situational Attitude Scale represents the use of quantified data so as to reduce racism.

6. *Find ways of involving minority students' parents in school affairs.* We found that black parents had virtually no contact with a school that was having trouble between its black and white students. The white principal said he had tried everything, to no avail. ("Everything" included announcements and handouts in school and letters to the homes.) We got in touch with the parents of one black student, arranged a meeting with them at their home, and found them quite interested—but not participating—in school affairs. First, the

PTA meetings were held in the evening, when they and many other black parents worked. Second, when they *did* come to PTA meetings, they were in such a small minority that they were reluctant or afraid to raise issues related to black students. We also found that the best time for a meeting of black parents was early morning.

After checking with school officials, we asked these two black parents to help us recruit others, which they did. The school did its part, with a phone call to all the black parents. So a meeting of black parents, teachers, and administrators was held at six a.m. one Wednesday, and the participants got an earful of one another's concerns. The result was a permanent black parent–student advisory group. Among other things, the group held a special black parent orientation session (at a convenient time) and a black "career night" that focused on specific interests and needs of blacks.

Another point that had been overlooked by the school was the fact that many blacks in that area were stonemasons, a well-paying and highly skilled craft. Thus stonemasonry was highlighted in the program and, as a result, the school offered more vocational courses in stonemasonry. This is an example of a real benefit that the school had not tapped because the administration had not considered the cultural, racial, and vocational variables of either the children or the parents.

Minority parents are much more likely to feel alienated from a school than white parents. Therefore extra efforts, using cultural information, are called for.

7. *Make sure there is follow-up after a conference or workshop.* To accomplish this, we generally set up a working structure, or tie into an existing structure, to keep the project moving after we have officially finished our work in a school. The black parent group is an example of such a structure. In another case, preexisting departments in a high school report on antiracism activities each month.

Ideally, we space out our work in a school so we can pay visits after we have started something. In this way we can observe progress, and the teachers and administration know that we are coming back. We also tell them that we will be paying unofficial visits in the future. If this sounds pretty tame, remember that we are interested in change, not in being tough. But we have had to get tough on occasion.

In one school we suspected that the report we typically submit might be buried on the superintendent's desk, rather than used to spark interest and serve as a reference document for those in the conference. We therefore mailed copies to all the participants and asked several school board members and community leaders to write to us and request copies. Thus the report became a public document. The superintendent was furious, and said he would ban us from his district. We, in turn, said we would start a newspaper campaign against him and his lack of progress in eliminating racism if he didn't get moving. He relented and committed funds to some of the recommendations in the report. He did not welcome us in his district, but we still maintain contacts in a number of schools without his knowledge.

The media can be a very useful tool in campaigns against administrators, most of whom are more afraid of negative press coverage than seems warranted. However, this fear should be exploited. Most newspapers and radio and television stations welcome well-documented evidence of racism in the schools. Again, use the media wisely, but don't be afraid to use them when you must.

8. *Develop proper techniques for teaching standard English to black youngsters.* In-service training programs, staffed with black language experts, are called for here, and English teachers need particular work on methods of teaching standard English to students from various language or dialect backgrounds. All teachers, in fact, need special information

on how to understand and positively reinforce students in terms of their language or dialect.

9. *Achieve central administration support for positions that are taken to reduce or eliminate racism.*   It is important to have the open support of the top people for effective anti-racism efforts. "Open support" means written or public statements, as specific as possible, on the actions to be taken by a school. Aside from committing the top people, this will persuade some of the more cautious in the organization to get involved.

A university president who was reluctant to be specific about progress in eliminating racism would say only that such a report, prepared by the university senate, was being implemented. However, a group of students and faculty took the report and identified which offices should be involved in implementing the various changes. We then made appointments with each administrator and asked specific questions about progress. (Most of them did not even realize they had such responsibility.) We followed each meeting with a summary letter and asked for corrections within a week, or we would assume that our summary was correct. We were now ready to take on the president, although he avoided several meetings with us. But eventually he ran out of excuses, so we got our meeting.

The press was alerted and we brought a campus newspaper reporter with us. (Most large newspapers have campus "stringers"—part-time reporters who are eager for a crack at a good story.) We proceeded through the report, asking about progress on each point. When the president gave general answers, we countered with specific questions and answers, and several times forced him to back down on his previous statements (we knew more about the report and the progress than he did). He reluctantly agreed to a number of our points, and also agreed to issue a statement in support of the report. On *live man is worth ten dead ones"* as he fired his pistol. Rockwell volunteered in 1927 that Arnold preceded this retort with the words *"Not yet, daddy."* Case, however, attributed these remarks to Arnold after he had left the scene. On the other hand, eyewitness David Waterbury of Stamford, without reference to any repartee between Arnold and his attackers, reportedly only **"saw Arnold as he left his fallen horse taking his pistols with him."**[38] Likewise, Jared Sparks' balanced 1849 Arnold biography fails to include any conversation as the general wriggled free of his mount.

Other accounts claim that Arnold was not alone when he fell, and that either Captain Bell (presumably the wounded Jesse Bell of Stamford's Middlesex Parish) or 5th Connecticut Regiment Private Ebenezer Patchen of Redding was at his side. Redding historian William Grumman even claimed in 1904 that Patchen reputedly *"saved Arnold's life by presenting a musket at the breast of a British soldier about to fire at the General."* [39]

Arnold is then said by Rockwell to have *"made a flying leap over a six-barreled gate and escaped down a cow path on Stebbins' property."* Eyewitness James A. Holley, however, observed that after killing his adversary, Arnold **"walked deliberately off."**[40] Even the general's destination is disputed; some say he vanished into a nearby swamp, while other accounts claim Arnold rejoined his retiring command and tried to rally his men for another stand at Saugatuck Bridge in present day Westport. But Erskine's flanking force had already smashed the Rebel right wing and commanded the only accessible swamp, so the swamp-flight scenario can safely be assigned to hearsay.

Swamp flight or not, bayonet conversation or not, Tory pistol fatality or not, there can be no doubt that Benedict Arnold's star shone in battle that day at Ridgefield. Even his British adversaries begrudgingly recognized their opponent's courage. Writing three days later from the deck of the packet-ship *Mercury* in Long Island Sound, Captain G. Hutchinson observed:

> **Arnold escaped very narrowly with the loss of his horse, which was killed. Everybody said he behaved that day with uncommon resolution as to personal**

bravery, but did not give him much credit for his
judgment as a general.[41]

Barricade Breached

As the American main body withdrew, with or without
Benedict Arnold, local men sought shelter in neighboring
woods, or like 1st Ridgefield Militia Captain Ebenezer Jones,
returned to outlying farms to protect their homestead. Others
either surrendered or were forcibly taken, including Levi
Disbrow of Fairfield, the Mather brothers of Woodbury, and
New Yorkers Israel Chapman, James Crawford, and Newton
Crawford, presumably of Captain Lawrence's command.[42]

After overrunning the barricade, British troops
reformed ranks and secured the village. Because Benjamin
Stebbins was an avowed Tory, his provincial lieutenant son,
Josiah, was permitted to quash flames that spurted from the
shell-shocked dwelling. Stebbins' house was subsequently
commandeered as a temporary British field hospital whose
bloodstained floorboards remained visible until the building
was demolished. Old Ben Stebbins' granddaughter, Anna, is
said to have dressed the redcoat wounds. Although the
Stebbins house was knocked down in 1878 to make way for a
forty-room limestone mansion (also torn down less than a
century later), remains of the bullet-riddled front door may
still be seen today at Ridgefield's historic Keeler Tavern
Preservation Society Museum.

Before following Erskine's men in pursuit of the fleeing
Americans down Town Street, it is appropriate here to pause
a moment and examine the price paid for the British victory.
Oral tradition maintains the blood on Stebbins' floor was that
of a gallant young English officer who succumbed in the
flower of his youth, but Sir William Howe's formal report to
London clearly stated that no officers perished in the four-day
British incursion. Major Henry Hope of the 44th Foot *was*
wounded, probably during the ledge-scaling bayonet assault;
and the regiment suffered up to three killed and sixteen
wounded in their brave ascent. Three officers from the Irish
27th Foot (Major Conran, Captain Rutherford and Ensign
Mincin) were also hit, along with eleven rank and file, so it's
safe to assume that, together with Browne's provincials and

the 15th Foot (eight dead, seventeen wounded)[43] this Irish
Regiment enjoyed the honor of leading Tryon's barricade
assault. Most likely it was one of these Celtic or Yorkshire
lads whose lifeblood stained the Stebbins house floor for
another 101 years.

role as Royal Governor of New York. Having given up hope that a majority of Americans would turn Loyalist if treated gently, Tryon employed Hessian mercenaries on his next Connecticut visit, returning in 1779 to burn Fairfield virtually to the ground. His troops then torched half of Norwalk, and laid much of New Haven to waste. Poor health rendered Tryon inactive in 1780 and, gladly relinquishing his Governorship, he sailed to England in September of that year, never to return. His wife's fortune very much intact, Tryon entertained lavishly on the London social scene and, to his credit, actively helped numerous Loyalists, important and unimportant, who had suffered loss in America. Recognizing Tryon's thirty years of loyal service to the Crown, King George III bestowed the rank of lieutenant general in 1782. Although the ex-governor still fiddled administratively as colonel of his Canada-based 70th Regiment of Foot, he never returned to the field and died six years later. In his final years William Tryon regretted use of desolation warfare against coastal Connecticut, but his remorse came much too late to alter an American epitaph of ridicule and disgust.

Wooster, David (1711-1777). Spinal column severed, the general discovered early from his attending physicians that recovery was impossible. After three agonizing days of delirium, through which his wife sat often unrecognized at his bedside, Wooster died in Danbury on Friday, May 2nd. Instead of the hero's funeral he deserved, the Continental service's most senior brigadier, and ranking Connecticut state militia officer, was quietly interred in a nearby burial ground; mortification was too advanced to transport the remains home to New Haven. According to sixteen-year old attendee Miss Betty Porter (whose father was killed by British the previous Saturday), only six men were present for the funeral. Wooster's bloodstained sash and battle sword were then dispatched to Yale, where they were exhibited until stolen sometime after 1895.

Wooster's home was plundered in 1779 by Tryon's British and Hessian regiments as they burned and looted New Haven. In addition to the general's personal papers, the records of his father-in-law, former Yale College President Reverend Thomas Clapp, were also taken. Wife Mary survived rough treatment at British hands, only to finish her life in poverty. Wooster's son had gone over to the British early in the war (although there is no evidence he bore arms), and Mary wrote to General Washington in 1782, asking for a pardon, but the Commander-in-Chief penned a non-committal response.

After Wooster's death, Congress voted a monument, but it was never erected, nor did Wooster's fellow soldiers or the State of Connecticut provide for a memorial marker of any kind. Three-quarters of a century passed before the Brotherhood of Masons remedied this embarrassing oversight. Twenty-seven years before his death, David Wooster had founded Connecticut's first Masonic lodge, the Hiram Lodge No. 1 of New Haven, of which he was elected the first master. His brothers never forgot! On April 27, 1852, seventy-five years to the day after his wounding, his brother masons of New Haven relocated the old general's remains to Wooster Cemetery in Danbury, and two years later erected the monument that stands today. According to James Case's 1927 account, 10,000 people attended the dedication, including Governor Charles H. Pond and two of his predecessors in office.

IX. Tryon's Trail Today

Two and a quarter centuries after His Majesty's last red-clad grenadier clambered aboard ship off Compo Beach, Ridgefield has transformed from a 1,708-soul backwater into a 24,000-person suburb anchoring the northern fringe of New York City's commuter belt. Yet, the rolling stonewall-laced ridges, twisting back roads, and third growth deciduous forests of the local landscape might appear familiar to General William Tryon and his Scottish engineer, Captain Archibald Robertson, should they ever pass this way again. For starters, the primary road network is little changed, and much of Tryon's route between Danbury and Ridgefield is still bordered by open space. Pine Mountain, Barlow Mountain, Mamanasco Lake, and Asproom Ledges still dominate the northern landscape, while glorious mile-long Main Street continues its broad swath through the village center. And perhaps most satisfying of all, 48 pre-Revolutionary dwellings identified by the Bicentennial Landmark Commission in 1976 remain standing, more than twenty of which still overlook Tryon's path through Ridgefield.

Facades jutting out like George Washington's determined jaw, these hand-hewn-oak post and beam structures reach across centuries to remind us of the builders' toughness and integrity. One wonders if their simple, honest lines and confident silhouettes gave passing British officers pause to reflect upon the character of the farmer militia closing in on their retreating column. After all, men who raised such erect, square-shouldered, no-nonsense homesteads might just put up a fight!

Tryon, Wooster and Arnold are, of course long gone, but the faint residue of Tryon's trail — dwellings, roads, natural landmarks, human stories — continues to beckon. As we re-trace this route today, we'll visit twenty-two buildings that witnessed passing British and American troops in April 1777. Several other houses that may have preceded the redcoat visit have been reluctantly omitted, alas, because of elusive provenance, or compromised architectural integrity.

Our journey begins at the Stephen Norris House just inside the Danbury border, proceeds west along the George Washington Highway (so-named after the general's 1780 traverse on his way from Peekskill to Hartford) to Ridgebury center, and then follows Ridgebury Road southward to North Salem Road. We'll take North Salem Road (Route 116) south to Benedict Arnold's barricade, traverse Town Street (Main Street) to Timothy Keeler's Tavern, and exit Ridgefield to the south via Wilton Road West. *Figure Nine* on the following page serves as our road map, identifying each surviving structure by the name of its 1777 owner.

After freeing their cannon from Miry Brook's muddy grasp, the King's soldiers entered Ridgefield shortly after dawn Sunday morning of April 27th, and began the two-mile slog over roller-coaster hills through Ridgebury Parish. Looming ahead immediately on the right was the late colonial homestead of Stephen Norris. Registered as a State Historic Building since 1969, the sturdy clapboard structure was erected a quarter-century before 1762, when John Norris sold half the dwelling to his son Stephen. Three years later Stephen married Abigail Keeler and, following their fifth child in 1774, acquired the remaining half from his father. (Did the bumper crop of children drive the grandparents to seek quieter quarters?) A sixth child had arrived by the time British soldiers appeared, and thirty-eight-year-old Stephen Norris must have had his hands full for there is no record that he actually bore arms during the War. Still, Norris was clearly in the Patriot camp, for town meeting records show him assigned by local freemen to a manpower procurement committee for filling Ridgefield's quota in Continental and State service.

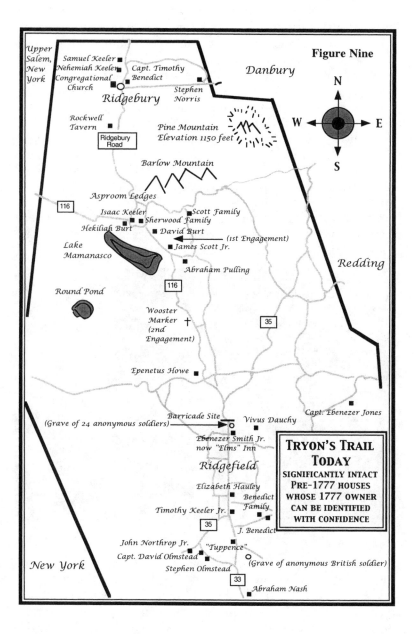

Upper Salem, New York

Samuel Keeler ■
Nehemiah Keeler ■   Capt. Timothy Benedict ■
Congregational Church ■
○ *Ridgebury*   Stephen Norris ■

Danbury

Figure Nine

Rockwell Tavern ■
┌─────────────┐
│ Ridgebury   │
│ Road   │
└─────────────┘

Pine Mountain Elevation 1150 feet

N
W ─── E
S

Barlow Mountain

Asproom Ledges

┌─────┐
│ 116 │
└─────┘
Isaac Keeler ■   Scott Family ■
■ Sherwood Family
Hekiliah Burt ■   ■ David Burt   ← (1st Engagement)
Lake Mamanasco   ■ James Scott Jr.

Abraham Pulling ■

Redding

┌─────┐
│ 116 │
└─────┘

Round Pond

Wooster Marker ✝ (2nd Engagement)

┌─────┐
│ 35 │
└─────┘

Epenetus Howe ■

Capt. Ebenezer Jones ■

(Grave of 24 anonymous soldiers) ──→ ○ Barricade Site   Vivus Dauchy ■
Ebenezer Smith Jr. now "Elms" Inn ■

Ridgefield

Elizabeth Hauley ■
■ Benedict Family
Timothy Keeler Jr. ■
┌─────┐
│ 35 │
└─────┘
J. Benedict ■

┌──────────────────────┐
│   **TRYON'S TRAIL** │
│   **TODAY**   │
│ SIGNIFICANTLY INTACT │
│ PRE-1777 HOUSES   │
│ WHOSE 1777 OWNER   │
│ CAN BE IDENTIFIED   │
│ WITH CONFIDENCE   │
└──────────────────────┘

John Northrop Jr. ■
Capt. David Olmstead ■   "Tuppence" ■
Stephen Olmstead   ○ (Grave of anonymous British soldier)

New York

┌─────┐
│ 33 │
└─────┘
Abraham Nash ■

Tryon's redcoats filed past the Norris place without halting, although minor pilfering may have taken place since Norris later claimed reimbursement for more than £4 in damages. Another scarlet-and-white-clad troop *did* pause for water and rest on July 1, 1781. This contingent, 4,800-strong, was part of Rochambeau's French army bound south to rendezvous with George Washington and immortality at Yorktown. Abigail Norris is said to have delivered a son that very day, and Comte de Rochambeau, so the story goes, requested the infant be named in honor of his aide, the Duc de Lauzun.[1]   Although no such Norris birth appears in Ridgefield town records, Norris descendants claim the Duc's French name remained in the family for generations, and town vital records do indeed reveal that, seventy-four years after Rochambeau's visit, Abigail's great-grandson "Delazon" Norris perished at the age of nine.

The circa-1740 House of Stephen Norris

More than a mile to the west, George Washington Highway terminates at Ridgebury Road to form the center of Ridgebury Parish — still a blissful little crossroad with half a dozen dwellings clustered around the Congregational Church. Originally sited on the coach route to Danbury, eighteenth-century Ridgebury was equipped with more taverns and inns than its small size might merit. The Fairchild Inn, Rockwell Inn, Doolittle Tavern and Nehemiah Keeler Tavern all eked out a trade along Ridgebury Road in 1777, and parts of both the Rockwell and Keeler structures still stand. Sadly, the rural farmland left to us by these tavern owners is rapidly transitioning to single-family-home subdivisions, so this peaceful setting will soon be permanently disrupted.

Listed on the National Register of Historic Places since 1984, the present Congregational Church dates from 1852, but a decidedly similar predecessor was erected on this site in 1769 when patriotic Reverend Samuel Camp and eighteen followers enlarged the New Patent Meeting House to create a "Second Ecclesiastical Society." The current structure presents a classic combination of Colonial and Greek-revival architectural styles. Particularly pleasing is the front gable with its completely returned pediment in the "Greek Temple" style, and front entry flanked by Doric pilasters and a pair of tall triple twenty-five-pane-sash windows — topped off by a purely Colonial bell tower.

The circa-1852 Congregational Church of Ridgebury

The burying ground (about 150 yards north of the church) housed only ten residents when British forces passed through in 1777, and had not witnessed a funeral since thirty-nine-year-old Sarah Coley departed this earth in November 1775. Today the yard is filled to capacity with more than 400 vanished souls, including little nine-year-old Delazon Norris, but the picturesque cemetery still emanates a solemn aura of bygone days.   Worth a look, the yard hosts seventeen Revolutionary War veterans, several who faced Tryon, along with French & Indian War Captain Timothy Benedict who met his maker in 1801, aged eighty-one.

Ridgebury Cemetery

Directly across the street from the church is Captain Benedict's circa-1750 homestead. If the story of gunshots from passing redcoat soldiers is to be believed, it was in this house that a Benedict girl quickly pulled her head away from an upper window amidst a shower of musket balls. The house itself, atop its fieldstone foundation, is now an oyster-colored church parsonage, much altered from Benedict's day.

About a half mile north along Ridgebury Road stands one of the jewels in Ridgefield's architectural crown — the circa-1717 Jonah Keeler House. When Tryon marched through Ridgebury in 1777, Jonah Keeler's large roadside dwelling had descended to son Samuel, described in family records as "ensign," despite any proven record of military

service.   Known as the "Pink House" for its traditional
exterior color, Jonah Keeler's five-bay, center-chimney
(crumbling original brick stack intact) "saltbox" still remains
in the Keeler family, a rare record of continuous ownership
encompassing more than 280 years!   Clad in hand-riven
chestnut shingles, with dentil molding beneath the eaves, and
displaying rare early-stage projecting gables, this superb
example of a third-stage colonial farmhouse is the oldest
surviving building in Ridgebury.

The circa-1717 "Pink House" of Samuel Keeler

There is no doubt that General Washington spent the
night of September 18, 1780 in Ridgebury. His Excellency is
said to have visited Samuel Keeler's nearby inn, but there is
no evidence he lodged under Keeler's roof. Samuel's brother
Nehemiah also operated a Ridgebury tavern (see *Figure
Nine*), and since Nehemiah fought with the 16th Connecticut
Militia at the Battle of Ridgefield, it's not farfetched to
imagine Washington dawdling that September eve to quench
his thirst and trade war stories with Alexander Hamilton and
other aides in the taproom of this still existing structure.

From Ridgebury southward to Old Stagecoach Road,
the rolling fields and abandoned orchards offer a glimpse of
the area's agricultural past, despite encroaching tract-home

subdivisions. After descending the twisting Asproom Ledges to meet North Salem Road, Tryon's men would have noticed a large center-chimney, five-over-four fenestrated farmhouse just ahead. Reputedly then occupied by one Hekaliah Burt of the predominantly Loyalist Burt family, this circa-1760 dwelling is still shingled in the weathered unpainted fashion typical of colonial days. Together with mature planting fields, farm pond, plethora of barnyard fowl, and handsome outbuildings, the complex to the rear provides the feel of a working farm, although both magnificent barns date to early in the twentieth century.

The reputed circa-1760 Home of Hekaliah Burt

A hundred yards southward, North Salem Road crosses Buffalo Creek, a meandering deep-gullied outlet from Lake Mamanasco that once powered a thriving mill trade. Loyalist Daniel Sherwood and his Patriot counterpart Isaac Keeler worked neighboring mills along this stream for more than a generation before the Revolution, but the sixty-two-year-old Keeler helplessly watched his gristmill set to flame by British soldiers the morning of Sunday, April 27, 1777. A circa-1830 Greek-revival residence presently on this site later rose from the wreckage of Keeler's mill, and is said to incorporate many original timbers. Although Isaac Keeler's millpond and dam were washed away by hurricane in 1955, remains of the saw, grist, and cider mills are still visible, while across the road to the west a reedy marsh engulfs the millpond basin.

Thankfully, Isaac Keeler's 1734 saltbox homestead just south along North Salem Road remains basically intact, although the structure was extended to the right in 1790, the roof raised in a late nineteenth century enlargement, and fireplace moved to an outside wall during the 1930's when an "ell" was added to the rear. Even so, an inside beehive oven, old hardware and latches, and a few millstones still remain from Keeler's day.

Isaac Keeler's circa-1734 Saltbox

Directly south of the Keeler house stands another dwelling that escaped Tryon's wrath — the circa-1750 residence of the Loyalist Sherwood family. Like his father before him, Daniel Sherwood Jr. was a miller, and like the Burts, fled with his family to Nova Scotia in 1780 following the Ridgefield freemen's vote to ban Tories from returning to town. The dual fieldstone chimneys are typical late colonial (1750-1775) architectural features affordable by prosperous tradesmen, and two old millstones still function as doorsteps. Much altered in external appearance (gable-roofed porch supported by Tuscan pillars, Chippendale sidelights, casement windows, and third-story dormers) the building was reputedly the site of Elias Read's 1783 store, and may have also been a stagecoach stop.

In 1765 Isaac Keeler deeded a twenty-eight acre parcel to his son Josiah, who erected the fine Colonial dwelling pictured below. More than two centuries later, the asymmetrical second story fenestration and striking side-light-flanked hooded entry porch still catch the eye. But if the porch existed in 1777, it would have been filled with wellwishers waving white handkerchiefs in support of the Crown when Tryon's column paraded by, for the house then belonged to Tory David Burt. Three years later, Burt absconded to the British, and the place was confiscated by the state. From mid-19th century through WWI this splendid 28' x 38' shingled farmhouse was owned by the Town of Ridgefield and operated as "Town Farm," a temporary home for down-on-their-luck locals who for whatever reason had no where else to live. Residents farmed the property and earned room and board by marketing the fruits of their field labor.

The circa-1765 Josiah Keeler House

Proceeding south on North Salem Road, we now cross into a section of Ridgefield known in Tryon's time as Scott's

Ridge. Originally populated by descendants of early silversmith James Scott, virtually every dwelling in the district was erected by the Scott family — ergo its later appellation as the Scotland District.

Around 1765, James Scott Jr. built one of the district's early homes at the junction of Barlow Mountain and North Salem roads. Now hidden behind tall twenty-first-century dry-laid fieldstone walls, it is one of Ridgefield's finest period saltboxes. Dubbed "saltboxes" because they resembled similar-shaped storage containers employed by farmwives to store precious salt, buildings like this started out as symmetrical rectangles, but were extended to the rear as more children arrived. This superbly maintained textbook-example saltbox is distinguished by the unbalanced second-floor gable wall window placements and the sweeping, elongated roofline of the one-and-a-half story shed-roofed extension. Tradition has it that rusted chains found in the cellar were once used to manacle Revolutionary War prisoners. This colorful scenario smacks of fiction, but General Wooster stashed his British prisoners *somewhere* in this vicinity when resuming pursuit of Tryon; who's to say it wasn't right here.

James Scott Junior's exquisite circa-1765 Saltbox

    In fields to the northeast of Scott's homestead British troops halted for a late-morning meal. Any sentry posted along Barlow Mountain Road to the south would have fixed an admiring gaze upon the house of Abraham Pulling. Purportedly erected around 1735 by original Ridgefield proprietor Thomas Hyatt, this center chimney colonial was expanded sometime between 1750 and 1775 when a keeping room was created in a wing to the east. Dr. and Mrs. Joseph Cashman began a museum-quality restoration in 1952 that preserved the splendid interior wainscoting and fireplace paneling while decorating with painstakingly documented paint and fabric tones. Now known as the Pulling-Dikeman House, this magnificent privately-owned plum-colored dwelling was considered noteworthy in the 1979 Preservation Trust Inventory of Ridgefield's private historic properties, deserving status as "one of the best small house museums in New England." Abraham Pulling owned the place in 1777, and while his political persuasion escapes record, Rockwell tells of an Abel Pulling (likely Abraham's brother) who served with Captain Ebenezer Jones' 1st Militia Company during the Ridgefield engagement. Abraham himself is best remembered in town records for siring nine children with wives Susannah, Esther, and Mercy between 1779 and 1804! Mercy indeed!

The circa-1735 Pulling-Dikeman House

As the redcoats chased down several cows to butcher for regimental mess, General David Wooster's small American force was rushing down Barlow Mountain Road from the east. Slipping through the trees, Wooster's men would have passed another circa-1760 farmhouse (sans the out-of-character circa-1940 third floor) erected by the prolific Scott family. Built by one of the sons of David Scott, this was the long time residence of James Scott Junior's son Hezekiah, a weaver and saw-mill operator best remembered for superior whiskey and cider brandy he distilled from the pure waters of "Uncle Kiah's Brook."

The circa-1760 home of Hezakiah Scott

After repulsing Wooster's surprise attack, the British resumed their southward march down North Salem Road. About a mile and a half from Ridgefield center, Wooster struck again. This time His Majesty's soldiers were not surprised, having readied a trio of cannon for the next American assault. Reputedly shot by a Tory sniper, Wooster slumped from his horse alongside the North Salem Road, mortally wounded. To mark the spot, a small granite memorial was installed on the west side of the road between two massive chestnut trees in 1896 by the Connecticut Masonic Lodge in memory of their fallen brother mason.

Today, the twin chestnuts have long since vanished, but the weather-beaten marker still reminds us of Wooster's sacrifice. It reads:

PLACE WHERE
WOOSTER FELL
DAVID WOOSTER
FIRST MAJ. GEN
OF THE CONN. TROOPS
IN THE ARMY OF THE REV.
BRIG. GEN. OF THE UNITED COL.
BORN AT STRATFORD
MARCH 2, 1710-11
WOUNDED ON THIS SPOT,
APRIL 27, 1777 . . .
WHILE DEFENDING THE
LIBERTIES OF AMERICA
AND NOBLY DIED AT
DANBURY MAY 2, 1777
GIVE ME LIBERTY OR GIVE
ME DEATH PATRICK HENRY
PRESENTED JULY 4 1806
BY E.A. HOUSEMAN OF DANBURY

The circa-1725 Epenetus How(e) House

After passing several eighteenth-century farmhouses along North Salem Road, whose histories have unfortunately defied verification, travelers are rewarded with the circa-1725 structure in which Loyalist Epenetus How(e)'s twin daughters were reputedly blessed (or damned) by British officers before Benedict Arnold's Town-Street barricade was assaulted. Perched above what was then a busy commercial site along the Titicus River, How(e)'s dwelling would have looked out over a series of small mills as well as his own felting and hat-making facility. Exceptional for chimney placements directly at gable-end in the Dutch Hudson River Valley fashion (as opposed to the English style of placing chimneys several feet farther in from the gable), the building is of both historical and architectural importance. Take a closer look at the two chimneys, the meticulously squared stones of which are tightly laid with little mortar. A recess in the attic floor chimney, large enough to hold several people, is reputed to have been a "Tory Hole."

Between Arnold's infamous barricade and Timothy Keeler's tavern a mile to the south, little remains completely intact of Revolutionary Ridgefield except for the circa-1713 home of original proprietor and Congregational Reverend Thomas Hauley (Hawley). Yes, core sections of the early eighteenth-century dwellings of Joseph Keeler (original proprietor lot #19) and Matthew Seamore (original proprietor lot #20) still survive along historic Town (Main) Street, but as entrancing as they may be, the current buildings date mostly from post-revolutionary times. The present-day Elms Inn, for example, occupies the pre-revolutionary foundation and frame of Ebenezer Smith Jr.'s circa-1760 homestead, but its five-over-four-fenestrated early Federal (1790) facade dates to first innkeeper Thomas Rockwell, and the long porch is late Victorian.

Reverend Hauley's house (original proprietor lot #5) witnessed Silliman and Arnold's outnumbered little army as it withdrew through Ridgefield, hotly pursued by Tryon's red-coated professionals. Listed in the Library of Congress Collection of Historic American Buildings, the structure is a rare and precious example of the Dutch Hudson River Valley influence, complete with original dormers, steep gambrel roof and overshoot "stoep" entry porch roof. Some interior doors are still painted in "faux-bois" wood graining, the alleged work of a Native American craftsman hired by Reverend Hauley. Unfortunately the artist reportedly disappeared on a drunken rampage and the project was never completed.

Reverend Hauley's circa 1713 residence, with well to the left

The Harvard-educated Hauley rendezvoused prematurely with his God at the age of forty-seven in 1739, and by 1767 the house had passed to Thomas Junior's wife Elizabeth.   During the Revolution, Elizabeth Hauley dispatched five sons to aid the Patriot cause, at least one of which, Elisha, fought in the Battle of Ridgefield. Perhaps Elisha even ducked inside his mother's house for cover as the British surged through town. Supposedly the charred beams in the south parlor corner near the entry porch are the mark of British torches, but more likely Silvio Bedini got it right in his 1958 *Ridgefield in Review*, when he noted the beams were charred on the inside, probably due to a domestic mishap.

It was no accident that our next house was set on fire by British soldiers for, as we discovered earlier, Timothy Keeler Junior's Tavern was clearly a center of Patriot resistance. Whatever his motives, Keeler's Loyalist neighbor (Benjamin Hoyt) may be thanked for saving this glorious structure by persuading Tryon to smother the flames. Unlike most pre-revolutionary homes, Keeler's gable-end fronts Town Street and the main entry door opens onto what then was a splendid view of the old village green. Barely twenty-one years old, Timothy Keeler Jr, occupied the newly built house in 1769 along with his new wife and fourteen-year-old "Negro-slave Betty." Five years later, Keeler opened his tavern to the public. Renowned architect Cass Gilbert added a new wing to the east in 1907, but the original core structure is still easily distinguished.

Timothy Keeler Junior's Tavern

Saved from an uncertain fate in 1965 by a group of public-spirited citizens, the tavern was restored to period state, earning both Connecticut and National Historic Building status, and functions today as one of New England's leading period museums, complete with Timothy Keeler's original tavern sign and several pieces of his household furniture. In addition to the well-known British cannonball still lodged in a corner post, the tavern houses three other important souvenirs from Tryon's Ridgefield visit:

- Captain Archibald Robertson's original hand-drawn map of the expedition.

- The only known surviving copy of James Sharpe's 1780 etching of Arnold's battlefield heroics, entitled "A Skirmish in America, between the King's Troops and Genl. Arnold."
- A bullet-riddled door from Benjamin Stebbins' old house that anchored the right wing of the American barricade.

Directly south of Keeler Tavern stands the Hoyt house. Erected by original proprietor and wealthy Norwalk merchant Benjamin Hoyt, the property passed to his two sons David and Benjamin Jr. when Hoyt Sr.'s will was probated in 1759. Benjamin Jr., fresh from incarceration in Fairfield for his Tory behavior, occupied the place in April 1777. While Hoyt's house was undoubtedly the most lavish in town during the Revolution, the massive, intricately detailed Georgian/High Federal-revival structure reigning on this site today, with its imposing third-floor Palladian window and ten-foot-tall first floor ceilings, seems too ostentatious for a country residence of the period. If Hoyt's home were nearly this grand in 1777, there is little wonder he interceded with General Tryon to prevent Keeler Tavern sparks from blowing his direction.

Two other dwellings that once graced Town Street in April 1777 have been subsequently moved to nearby locations: the circa-1740 David Scott House, and the old trading post, commonly known as "Tuppence."

The circa-1740 David Scott House displays fine "bones" at its new site

Then home of seventy-two-year-old French and Indian War captain Vivus Dauchy, the David Scott House stood at the intersection of Catoonah Street and Town Street, just north of the Episcopal Church burned by Tryon's men. While there is no record Dauchy actually fought at the barricade with Arnold, the virile Patriot certainly possessed sufficient energy to have done so, having sired 13 children (with three wives), the last of which at age 61! Facing demolition in 1999, the Scott House was saved for posterity by a group of concerned citizens who raised the money to dismantle and reassemble the structure at Grove Street and Sunset Lane as home to the newly founded Ridgefield Historical Society. Resplendently sheathed by authentically reproduced 32-inch shingles secured with rose-head nails, the venerable post and beam saltbox still retains most of its original broad oak floorboards.

Distinguished by its Hudson River Valley Dutch overhanging roofline, "Tuppence" (also known as Lannon House) was once a trading post, or small store, that evolved from a series of attached shacks. The structure originally stood on Town Street to the north of today's Town Hall, but substantially destroyed by fire the surviving frame was rehabilitated as a dwelling, then moved to its present site around 1940. The "Tuppence" name remains a mystery. Does it refer to the two-penny property tax levied by the Connecticut General Assembly during colonial times, or perhaps the dejected owners assessment of its value after the fire?

The area where High Ridge Road joins West Lane must have been a hotbed of Patriot activity in 1777, for three of the six Ridgefield dwellings torched by Tryon's minions lay nearby — the respective homes of Benjamin Northrop, John Northrop, and either Daniel Smith or Sarah Morehouse. John Northrop Jr. may even have witnessed the destruction of his father's house, for his own residence was less than a hundred yards away! Erected by Benjamin Rockwell around 1740, this one-and-a-half-story clapboard structure, with its classic beehive oven inside the main fireplace, passed into the younger Northrop's hands in 1755. Now an antiques shop, the core building provides a classic illustration of early colonial domestic construction.

"Tuppence"

The circa-1740 house of John Northrop Jr.

After burning the Northrop houses, a detachment of
Tryon's force turned south down Olmstead Lane, where at
least four Olmstead dwellings lay, three of which survive

today. The first, at the southwest corner of West and Olmstead Lanes, evidences several Victorian and twentieth-century alterations, but down Olmstead Lane on the right, the Captain David Olmstead House remains in wonderful condition. Captain Olmstead, it may be recalled, was one of the first Ridgefielders to bear arms, and was present at the Battle of Ridgefield, even if he had vanished to a woodland hiding place when his resourceful wife allegedly flashed her petticoats from an upstairs window to save the structure from British torches.

Captain David Olmstead's circa-1760 farmhouse

If the so-called "red petticoat" story is to be believed, this is most likely the house from which Abigail Olmstead displayed her scarlet wares. Although the place was not burned, it was apparently severely plundered, for a reimbursement request exceeding £54 appears under Captain Olmstead's name on the summary of damages submitted by town selectmen to the General Assembly. Resting on a dry-laid stone foundation and rich in original details, this modest little eye-brow-windowed farmhouse, despite its Federal hooded porch, represents the typical Revolutionary-era residence both in size and simplicity.

Across the street is another pre-Revolutionary dwelling, most likely the 1777 home of militia captain Josiah Hine. Originally a mirror image of Captain Olmstead's house, this circa-1750 center-chimney colonial' roofline is unfortunately marred by a pair of hipped dormers that superseded original eyebrow windows around 1910. Happily, many original features still distinguish the interior — a stone fireplace with beehive oven and iron hardware, batten doors, wide floorboards, and pegged windows. Formerly owned by mid-nineteenth-century carriage-trade blacksmith W.W. Seymour, the barn in the rear still contains an old forge.

Stepping back across Olmstead Lane, yet another modest eyebrow-windowed little house from Tryon's time awaits us about fifty yards to the south. This barn-red structure was then home to Stephen and Hannah Olmstead and their three teenaged sons. Stephen fought with Captain Ebenezer Jones' 1st Ridgefield Militia at the barricade with Silliman and Arnold and, like kinsman David Olmstead, also found safety in the surrounding trees after the engagement. Somehow, though, Hannah saved this house without displaying any undergarments. Or did she?

The circa-1740 Stephen Olmstead House

Having rid Olmstead Lane of any lingering Patriots, the redcoats halted on Wilton Road West (then known as the Norwalk Road for Wilton was not incorporated until 1802) until a similar flanking force completed its sweep along East Ridge. Following a spirited skirmish, this second contingent marched down Rockwell Road past two Benedict family residences to rejoin Tryon's main column.

The circa-1755 Benedict House

Remarkable for its end-bay door placement and asymmetrical four-over-four front facade fenestration, the bright-canary clapboard structure on the south side of narrow Rockwell Road as it twists westward is a well-maintained center-chimney saltbox. While the building itself is circa-1750, its 1777 owner J. Benedict remains a mystery since there were two James Benedicts, two Josephs, two Johns and one Josiah Benedict in town at the time. The large original barn collapsed in 1947, burying a 1903 Franklin automobile, which reportedly remains entombed to this date.

Across Rockwell Road stands another of Ridgefield's most cherished antique structures, the circa-1730 residence and attached cobbler's shop of French and Indian War Ensign James Benedict. Tradition tells us the inhabitants were British Loyalists during the Revolution, and had painted their chimney-top white to alert Crown soldiers to spare the house. Patriot militia reportedly engaged Tryon's redcoats at the top of the hill (where Rockwell Road joins Branchville Road) and British casualties were supposedly cared for under this roof. Faithfully restored by noted architect Cass Gilbert for one of his daughters in the 1920's, this picturesque property is protected today by the Ridgefield Historic District Commission.

The "Cobbler's House" of Ensign James Benedict

Tryon's flanking detachments rejoined his main column to encamp for the night of April 27, 1777 just below the original town burying ground between today's Wilton Road West and Wilton Road East. Next morning the British broke camp at dawn and proceeded down Wilton Road West (the "Old Norwalk Road") toward their awaiting ships... and safety. Several South Ridgefield dwellings that may have witnessed the march still stand today, but only one — the Joseph Osborne House — can be traced with certainty to Tryon's time, although the building was moved about a hundred feet back from the road in 1963.

Erected by Osborne around 1730, this majestic 39'x29' center-chimney colonial is distinguished by beaded, weathered clapboards secured by rose-head forged nails. By

1741 Osborne's six-acre lot had grown to 20 acres, complete with barn and orchard, but new owner Daniel Chapman (namesake son of the long-time Greens Farms Congregational Church minister) apparently encountered financial difficulty and mortgaged the place to wealthy Boston merchant John Dennie.   Chapman never retired the mortgage, and when Dennie departed this earth in 1760, his descendants dealt the property to twenty-year old Abraham Nash.

The circa-1730 house of Abraham Nash

Fervid Patriot during the Revolution, Nash was reputedly one of only nine Ridgefield freemen to vote for "Congress" instead of "King" in the controversial town meeting of January 1775 when Ridgefield chose to remain loyal to King George III. When the town finally switched to the American cause in December 1775, Nash was one of twenty-six Patriots named to the "committee of inspection" to ferret out local Tories and persuade them to take the oath of allegiance. Although Nash cannot be placed with certainty at the Ridgefield barricade during Tryon's attack, his name appears with the rank of sergeant in Captain Hine's company of Colonel Nehemiah Beardsley's 16th Connecticut Militia regiment in 1779. At that stage in the War, some measure of experience was necessary in a sergeant, so it's quite likely

Nash saw action sometime between 1776 and 1779. In any event, Sergeant Nash responded with his unit to the subsequent alarms at Fairfield, Bedford, and Norwalk.

We can be sure that Nash was elsewhere when the British column retreated past his front door just after sunrise on the morning of April 28, 1777, for Loyalist informers (such as Town Street resident Ezekiel Wilson, who accompanied Tryon all the way to Saugatuck Bridge) would surely have given him away... and perhaps torched this fine house in the process.

And so we come at last to the end of Tryon's Ridgefield trail. No matter how hard we try; no matter how much imagination or nostalgia we summon; no matter how deeply we hunger for *just one more glimpse* at the ragtag militia of farmers, tradesmen, patriotic old men, and excited teen-agers who faced King George's professionals, they shall never pass this way again. Yet as we have seen, many of their homes still stand. Square-shouldered, honest, unpretentious, these galleons of the land have leaned head-on for more than two centuries into the worst that nature could hurl their way. And yet still they stand! In Ridgefield, throughout Connecticut, and across New England, these wooden monuments bear lasting witness to our glorious Revolutionary heritage. Treasure them, oh reader, for someday, like Wooster, Arnold, Silliman, and Tryon, they too shall be gone.

Appendix A

1.) Letter from Brigadier General Benedict Arnold to Brigadier General Alexander McDougall, from Saugatuck, 28 April 1777. The Papers of the Continental Congress, 1774-1789. M247, roll 167, item 152, vol. 4, pp. 145-47.

Saugatuck, 3 Miles E.t Norwalk
28th April, 1777, 6 o'clock P.M.

Sir:

Soon after I wrote you yesterday I found the Enemy were on their march for Ridgefield.— At 11 o'Clock we arrived there about one hour before them with 500 men. We had little time to make a disposition of our troops, when a smart action began which lasted about one hour.— Our troops were obliged to give way to superior numbers; I found it impossible to rally them, & ordered a Stand to be made at this place at 11 o'Clock. This morning we met the Enemy with 500 Militia about two miles from this place when a skirmishing began between the Flanks & soon became general, which continued until five o'Clock, when the Enemy gained an height under cover of their Ships, and embarked before Night. At the beginning of the action Col.o Huntington joined me with 500 Men, & before it was over a Small number of Gen.l Wadsworth's Brigade – Gen.l Wooster, whose conduct does him great honour, was mortally wounded yesterday.— Lieut. Col.o Gold killed, and Col.o Lamb wounded – our loss otherwise is not great, about twenty killed and wounded. [Many of the Officers and Men behaved well – The Militia as usual – I wish never to see another of them in action]. The Enemy's loss is uncertain, as they carried off most of their killed & wounded.— Several prisoners have fallen into our hands – as soon as the Troops were embarked the Fleet got under way and stood to the Eastward.— Extreme hurry & fatigue obliges me to request your advising His Excellency Gen.l Washington of the above matters.

I am very respectfully, Sir,
Yr. H---,
B. Arnold

Hon.able Gen.l McDougall

2.) Dispatch from Brigadier General Gold Selleck Silliman to Governor John Trumbull, Fairfield, 29 April 1777. Manuscript copy in the Fairfield Historical Society, believed to be in his own hand.

Sir:

Last Friday about half past Twelve I was informed that a Fleet of Shipping were close in with the land off Norwalk, on which I went on the Hill where the Enemy lately attempted to make a Descent. A little to the West of this Town, here I could see the Fleet, & as the wind was so they were obliged to beat it up, it was sometime before I was satisfied that they intended to stop here, but as soon as I was, I sent out immediately for all the Companies, in the 1ˢᵗ Regt. & for the rest of the Brigade to come in as fast as possible & sent also an Express to Genl. Wooster to acquaint him with it, & that the Fleet consisted of 24 sail in the whole 16 of them ships, at 5 o'clock P.M. This Fleet Anchored in Compo Bay, & immediately landed (as we compute this in our observation) About 2000 but the Prisoners we have taken say 4,000 Men commanded by Gen. Erskine, they immediately possessed themselves of Compo Hill. In the Evening We had intelligence that the Enemy were advanced some Way up toward the Country Road which was about 2 Mile, Distant upon this Lieut. Col. Dimon marcht with such of the Militia as were got in, being only about 50 with some 20 Continental Soldiers to Watch the Motion of the Enemy; this Party was posted along the Road from Greensfarms Meeting House to Saugatuck River; a small Skirmish happened this night between a few of this Party and the Enemy; Advanced 3 of the Enemy were badly wounded; One of them Deacon Lyman's Son who it is said is mortally wounded. Next Morning a little after Sun Rising we received advice that the Enemy were advancing to the Northward all the Militia that had got in were paraded, & Before we could move Advice came that the Enemy had turned their Course Northeast into the Danbury Road & that they were advancing up that way with great Rapidity & that they were then about 7 Miles ahead of us. And we immediately marched on after them to watch their Motions; being then only about 120 Men we marched off & pursued but could no come in Sight of the Enemy; at Redding we found our Forces was increased by about 600 Men; here we halted for a little Time to refresh the Soldier & then marched on still hoping to be able to get to Danbury, so as to be able to prevent Distruction of the publick Stores if possible; General Arnold joined me about 4 Miles below Redding, & General Wooster at Redding, about 12 o'clock at Night we arrived at Bethel 2 1/2 Miles South of Danbury exceedingly fatigued as the Roads were full of Mud & Water & the Night extremely dark. Here we found that we had come too late, & that the Town was then in Flames which continued all the Night – Next Day and I am informed by Capt. Lockwood who was on the Spot that about 36 houses were burnt, in the Night I received advice from Col. Huntington that he had retreated out of the Town on to the hill about 2 miles with most of the Division with about 50 Continental Troops & that he had been obliged at the Approach of the Enemy to Abandon the Town & the greatest part of the Stores at the same Time we received advice from Maj. Beardsly that he was on the hills to the Northeast with about 150 Men More; we immediately advised him of our numbers which about 600; next Morning at Day Light 400

Men under Command of Gen Arnold & myself marched & took post on the Road from Danbury down thru Wilton in Order to harass the Enemy on their Return as we had reason to believe they would return that way & Gen Wooster with the Remainder of our Troops was to harass their Rear. About 11 O'clock we received Advise that the Enemy were returning by the Road Thro Ridgefield, on this We directly paraded our Men & marched thro the Northwesterly part of Redding over to Ridgefield & took our post across the Ridgefield Town Street near the Church & formed a Small Breast Work of Rails Timber & across the Road & posted our small Body which was now increased to about 500; at this Work & at several other Posts along our Flanks that were important. We posted our Men & waited the coming of the enemy. Of their approach we had Notice by the Firing in the Enemies rear occasioned by Gen Woosters Harassing them in their Rear, Poor Gen Wooster in this Service received a Shott in his Body which Docr Turner Supposed to be mortal. About 3 O'clock the Enemy appeared in One grand column that filled the Road full for more than half a Mile in Length when their Front came within a half a Mile as they halted to make their Dispositions for the attack they began first by a Cannonade from 6 Field Pieces; This not answering their purpose they sent out large flanking Parties to flank us, they were received warmly by our out Posts, for a while, but the Enemy soon marched up a large collum containing about 600 Men right in our Front; and very large flanking Parties on each of their Flanks consisting either of them of more Men than Men our whole force consisted of, with 3 Field Pieces in the Front of their Collum; Upon this a hott Fire ensued from both Sides, which continued with great Fury for about half an hour more when we were obliged to give way to a Superior Force in this Action we lost Col. Gold killed & 8 or 9 others, but the Certainty of the matter I have not yet got we had several Wounded. The Enemy had a greater Number killed much more than we had; We were obliged to give way to a Superior Force as they were at least 4 to our One. The Enemy immediately set several Buildings on Fire, & we expected they would destroy not only that Town, but every other Place they came to in their way, for the greatest savages of Africa or America never marked their Way with such acts of Barbarity and Cruelty as these have done Murdering the wounded that fell in their hand with Circumstances of Cruelty that would Disgrace even Savage. After our Defeat Gen. Arnold & myself together concluded to endeavor to rally our scattered Forces, & at least keep the Enemy from plundering the whole Country through which they passed; accordingly Yesterday at 11 O'clock A.M. we took post on an Eminence near Saugatuck River, on Norwalk Side near the Bridge on the Road that we were informed the Enemy was marching down in; with about 700 Men whom we had collected with 2 Field Pieces; There we had not staid long before the Enemy appeared on a Eminence Advancing toward us near 2 Miles off, harassed in their Rear by Gen. Woosters Division; they marched on & formed for an Attack as they marched at the Distance of about 3/4 of a Mile, when we saw this we ordered a Six pound Shoot to be fired at them, & from their Behavior it was evident they did not expect it, they made a Halt; on which a Number mor were fired at them which seemed a little to confuse them; on the whole they relinquished the Idea of attacking us, & filed off to the Left until they came to Saugatuck River, about Two Miles above the Bridge & through that they waded & marched Down the East Side of the River, in order to get to their Ships observing this we Determined to cross the River at the Bridge,

& attack them in Flank as they Marched along and in order to strengthen ourselves to do it effectually we order the Division of Militia lately commanded by Gen. Wooster which lay back on the Hills about 2 miles off immediately to join us; & they being greatly increased in Number we formed the whole into two collums & pursued the Enemy as fast as we could but they got Down to the Shore before we overtook them, & there a Smart Skirmish for more than an Hour in Length Ensued in which Sundry Men were killed on both Sides & many wounded. During the whole Action the Enemy kept constant embarking & finished after the Action Ended, & a little before Sun Setting they came to Sail & left us, & went into Huntington & this Day all the Militia that was called in on this occasion were dismissed; Gen Wadsworth got in a little after the Action was over, part of his Brigade were here & in the Action. A particular Account of killed & wounded I have not got but the Dcr tells me he has dressed between 70 & 80 I am Your Honours Most Obed' & Most Hum'l

Ser'nt

G. Selleck Silliman.

The foregoing is a true copy of)
the Original as sent this Day)
to his Hon. Gov. Trumbull)

P.S. By the best Accounts I can get we lost in both Actions about 20 Men, & have as within 70 or 80 wounded; & the Enemy has about 40 killed that we know of, & how many more that they Carried we know not nor do we know about their wounded. General Arnold who is an Excellent Officer towards the close of the Action Could have killed & taken great Numbers of the Enemy that were engaged with his Division if he had not been at the critical minit deserted by the Men he commanded, which mortified him extremely a sensible young Officer that stood by and heard Gen. Arnold lament his Disappointment to their rejoice at it For he believed now that our General Assembly was to be convinced that our Militia was a Body of Men that could not be depended upon by reason of their not being inured to Duty, & I must say that I am fully of the Opinion, but upon being properly disciplined they are good men. We have taken at Different Posts sundry Prisoners, but how many I have not got the Acct. of. The Enemy Yesterday afternoon were off Morononeck & New Rochel.

3.) *Account of the Battle of Ridgefield in the personal journal of Captain Archibald Robertson, Royal Engineers. Diary, Book Two, 1777, From Harry Miller Lydenberg, ed., Archibald Robertson, Lieutenant General Royal Engineers, His Diaries and Sketches in America, 1762-1780 (New York: The New York Public Library, 1930), pp.127-29.*

[1777, April] 27ᵗʰ by Day break set fire to all the Stores and March'd about 8 o'clock on our Return to the ships by way of Ridgefield. Had information that the Rebels were Collecting in Numbers to oppose us and Mollest our Rear. The first that made their Appearance was on Ridgebury hill about five miles from Danbury. They fired on the Rear at a great Distance with little harm, When we got near Ridgefield we found General Arnold posted on the hills and in the Village with about 700 men and Generals Worcester and Sillyman in our Rear with about 400. We immediately (2 o'clock) Attack'd the Village and drove them off and took Possession. General Worcester at the same time attack'd our Rear but was repulsed. After being in the Village a little while the Rebels again drew together and came up to gain a Rising Ground above the Village, upon which Sir William Erskine made a Disposition to surround them. However by the different Companys now advancing at the same time, we only Dispersed then and drove them off. In three severe Skirmishes we had about 50 or 60 men Killed and Wounded and 4 or 5 Officers, Major [Henry] Hope, Captain Rutherford, etc. We lay near the Village all night, 4 Battalions in line and two on the Wings, i.e. one on each wing.

[April] 28ᵗʰ. At Day Break began our march. For 5 or 6 miles had only a few Popping Shots from behind Houses, Rocks etc. Were inform'd they intended to oppose us at Norwalk Bridge. However by a clever move to our left we pass'd another Bridge and got by them. Here we found Rum and other Stores in the Woods. When we got within 5 miles of the Shore we got upon a high hill call'd Chestnut hill, from which we could discern our Ships and the Rebels drawn up about 2 miles in front to oppose our Passing a Bridge over the Sauketuk River, but by another. Rapid and well conducted move we again Wheel'd to our left, pass'd the River at a Ford, and push'd two Battalions to the Bridge by which means the Rebels were shut in until all our Detachment pass'd by them in sight. Mr. Arnold endeavored to pass the Bridge but was not followed by his men. The 4ᵗʰ Regiment which defended the Bridge being call'd off, we march'd from hill to hill towards the water side, the Rebels pressing on our Rear and Appearing in Considerable Numbers, Skirmishing all the way. At last we reach'd Compo Hill near the beach where we were drawn up, and the Rebels advanced from Wall to Wall keeping up a very heavy fire of Musquetry and two pieces of Cannon. At length they came so near that it was thought advisable to charge them with fix'd Bayonets, which was done with 4 Regiments, the 4ᵗʰ, 15ᵗʰ, 23ʳᵈ, and 27ᵗʰ, and we drove them back a great way Killing considerable Numbers. After this they never more advanced and we embarked on board our ships without a Shot being fired. Our men very much fatigued by so Rapid and long a march. The Rebels appeared to me to be upwards of 4,000 men. Great praise is due to Sir William Erskine for his good Conduct on this Expedition. Tho' General Tryon and Brigadier General Agnew were both older, He ordered everything . . . Our Loss on the whole is about 140 Killed and Wounded and 14 Officers Wounded. The loss of the Rebels cannot be Ascertain'd but must be considerable.

[April] 29ᵗʰ. Landed at New York.

By a Return from the Rebels we learn that their Loss in the Last Expedition to Danbury was as follows 100 killed and 200 wounded, among the former one General Worcester and two Lieutenant-Colonels.

4.) Extract of a letter from the Hon. General Sir Wm. Howe, to Lord Geo. Germaine, dated New-York, April 30, 1777, received by the Mercury Packet.

I have now the   honour of reporting to your Lordship the success of that expedition, and to inclose a return of the stores destroyed.

The troops landed without opposition in the afternoon of the 25 th of April, about four miles to the Eastward of Norwalk, and 20 from Danbury.

In the afternoon of the 26 th the detachment reached Danbury, meeting only small parties of the enemy on their march; but Gen. Tryon having intelligence that the whole force of the country was collecting to take every advantage of the strong ground he was to pass on his return to the shipping, and finding it impossible to procure carriages to bring off any part of the stores, they were effectually destroyed; in the execution of which the village was unavoidably burnt.

On the 27th in the morning the troops quitted Danbury, and met with little opposition until they came near to Ridgefield, which was occupied by Gen. Arnold, who had thrown up entrenchments to dispute the passage, while Gen. Wooster hung upon the rear with a separate corps. The village was forced and the enemy drove back on all sides.

Gen. Tryon lay that night at Ridgefield, and renewed his march on the morning of the 28th. The enemy, having been reinforced with troops and cannon, disputed every advantageous situation, keeping at the same time smaller parties to harass the rear, until the General had formed his detachment upon a height within cannon-shot of the shipping, when the enemy advancing, seemingly with an intention to attack him, he ordered the troops to charge with their bayonets, which was executed with such impetuosity, that the rebels were totally put to flight, and the detachment embarked without further molestation.

. . . . Return of the stores, ordnance, provisions, &c. as nearly as could be ascertained, found at the rebels stores, and destroyed by the King's troops at Danbury &c. in Connecticut, April 27, 1777. A quantity of ordnance stores, with iron, &c. 4000 barrels of flour; 100 large tierces of bisket; 89 barrels of rice; 120 puncheons of rum.

Several large stores of wheat, oats, and Indian corn, in bulk, the quantity thereof could not possibly be ascertained; 30 pipes of wine; 100 hogsheads of sugar; 50 ditto of melasses; 20 casks of coffee; 15 large casks filled with medicines of all kinds; 20 barrels of saltpeter; 1020 tents and marquees; a number of iron boilers; a large quantity of hospital bedding, &c. engineers, pioneers, and carpenters tools; a printing-press compleat; tar, tallow, &c. 5000 pair of shoes and stockings.

At a mill between   Ridgeberry and Ridgefield: 100 barrels of flour, and a quantity of Indian corn. At the bridge at the West brace of Norwalk River, and in the woods contiguous: 100 hogsheads of rum; several chests of arms, paper cartridges; field forges; 300 tents.

Return of the killed, wounded, and missing: One drummer and fifer, 23 rank and file, killed; three field-officers, six captains, three subalterns, nine sergeants, 92 rank and file, wounded; one drummer and fifer, 27 rank and file, missing. Royal artillery. Two additionals killed; three matrosses, one wheeler, wounded; one matros missing.

(Signed) W. Howe.

4th regiment, Capt. Thorne, wounded, 15th, Capt. Dirmas, Lieut. Hastings, of the 12th regiment, acting as a volunteer, wounded. 27th, Major Conran, Capt. Rutherford, Ensign Minchin, wounded. 23rd, Second Lieut. Price, volunteer Vale, wounded. 44th, Major Hope, wounded. 64th, Capt. Calder, Ensign Mercer, wounded. Prince of Wale's American volunteers, Col. Browne, Capt. Lyman, Capt. Seon, wounded. 71st regiment, Capt. Simon Frazer, a volunteer, wounded.

Return of the Rebels killed and wounded.

Killed. Gen. Wooster, Col. Goold, Col. Lamb of the Artillery, Col. Henman, Dr. Atwater, a man of considerable influence, Capt. Cooe, Lieut. Thompson, 100 privates.

Wounded. Col. Whiting, Capt. Benjamin, Lt. Cooe, 250 privates.

Taken. 50 private, including several Committee-men.

Appendix B

Below is a roster of Americans who can be placed with certainty in Ridgefield with Generals Wooster, Arnold or Silliman on April 27, 1777. A single asterisk designates "killed" at Ridgefield, and two asterisks denote "wounded."

Name		Unit	Source
Abbott, Seth	Lt.	Wilton Militia	Hubbard
Atwater, David	Dr.		Hubbard, Case, Johnston, Rockwell, Howe, Robertson
Baker, Amos	Dr.		Rockwell
Bartlett, Joshua*		3rd Ct. Line	Rockwell, CT. Hist. Society Records of American Rev., Johnston
Beardsley, Nehemiah Maj.		16th Ct. Militia	Case, Debany, Johnston
Beers, Daniel			Rockwell
Belden, Azor Capt.		Wilton Militia	Rockwell, Hurd, Hubbard
Bell, Jesse Capt.**		9th Ct. Militia	Hubbard, Grumman, Wicks & Olsen, McDonald
Bell, Thaddeus		9th Ct. Militia	McDonald, Grumman, Wicks & Olsen
Bennett, Elias		4th Ct. Militia	Rockwell
Bennett, Najah Capt.		4th Ct. Militia	Bedini
Benjamin, John Col.**		4th Ct. Militia	Johnston, Rockwell, Bedini
Bostwick, Elisha		Wilton Militia	Hubbard
Bouton, Moses		Westchester Mil.	Van Norden
Bouton, Seth		1st Ridgefield Mil.	Rockwell
Bradley, Anan		New Haven	Grumman
Bradley, Philip B. Col.		5th Ct. Line	Records of the American Revolution, Series I, Vol.VII, Rockwell,Grumman, Johnston
Bradley, Levi			Welsh, Grumman
Bradley, Stephen R. Capt.		Wooster Staff	McDevitt, Rockwell

Buell, David	16th Ct. Militia	Rockwell
Bull, Daniel**	16th Ct. Militia	Hubbard, Grumman
Bunce, Isaiah **	7th Regiment	Clark
Cain, Hugh Ensign	16th Ct. Militia	Rockwell
Carter, John Capt.	Canann P. Militia	Bayles
Chapman, Israel		Rockwell, Johnston
Coe, Ebenezer Capt.**	4th Ct. Militia	Rockwell, Hubbard, Orcutt, Knapp,Grumman, Johnston, Wilcoxson, Howe, Robertson
Coggin (Cogins), David	5th Ct. Line	Ct. Hist. Soc. Collections, Johnston
Congo, Jack	5th Ct. Line	U.S. Army Records, Bedini
Cooke, Joseph P. Col.	16th Ct. Milita	Wilton Library Archives Benedict, Johnston,Bailey
Couch, Thomas		Johnston
Crane, Thaddeus Major**	4th Westchester Militia	Rockwell, Van Norden Keeler Family, Grumman
Crawford, James		Johnston
Crawford, Newton		Rockwell, Johnston
Curtis, Ephraim** Lt.	4th Ct. Militia	Hubbard, Wilcoxson
Curtis, William**	4th Ct. Militia	Clark
Darling, Joseph Lt.	1st Rfield Milita	Rockwell
Davenport, Hezekiah* Lt.	9th Ct, Militia	Grumman, Johnston, Orcutt, Wicks & Olsen, Clark,Bayles
Dean, Bradley*	5th Ct. Line	Betts, Johnston, U.S. Army Records
Dean, Jeremiah	5th Ct. Line	Betts, U.S.Army Records
Delavan, Timothy		McDonald, Bedini
DeForest, Uriah	9th Ct. Militia	Rockwell
Dibble, John		McDonald
Dimon, David Lt. Col.	6th Ct. Line	Sheftall, Grumman
Disbrow, Levi		Johnston
Drinkwater, William	16th Ct. Militia	Rockwell
Edmond, Robert	Farmer	Rockwell
Edmond, Robert**	13th Ct. Milita	Hubbard, Johnston
Edmond, William**	5th Ct. Line or 13th Ct. Militia	item # 3266, Keeler Tavern Archives, Rockwell, Johnston
Eells, John	Canaan P. Militia	Bayles
Fairchild, Stephen**	4th Ct. Militia	Grumman, Rockwell, Todd Hubbard,
Gold, Samuel** Sgt.	5th Ct. Line	Hubbard, Todd, Grumman
Gorham, Timothy	New Haven	Grumman
Goodsell, Lewis Lt.	4th Ct. Militia	Grumman
Gould, Abraham Col.*	4th Ct. Militia	Rockwell, Child, Schenk, Grumman, Johnston, Howe
Gregory, Ezra	Wilton Militia	Hubbard
Gregory, Matthew Lt.	Wilton Militia	Rockwell, Hubbard, Hurd
Gray, Nathan Lt.*	4th Ct. Militia	Rockwell
Haines, Silas*	4th Ct. Militia	Bedini
Hawley, Elisha	1st R-field Militia	Rockwell

Hawley, Robert**	4th Ct. Militia	Hubbard, Grumman
Hawley, William	4th Ct. Militia	Bedini, Grumman
Hill, Ebenezer Capt.	4th Ct. Militia	Grumman
Hinman, Benjamin** Col.	13th Ct. Militia	Johnston, Debany, Hubbard
Hinman, Joel**	Woodbury Militia	Root
Holley, James		McDonald
Holmes, John**	9th Ct. Militia	Huntington, Grumman
Holmes, Squire		Bedini
Husted, Nathaniel		Wicks & Olsen
Husted, Thaddeus	New York Militia	Bayles, Wicks & Olsen
Hull, Ezra	4th Ct. Militia	Todd, Grumman
Huntington, Jedediah Col.	1st CT. Line	McDevitt, Caulkins, Case
Hyde, Joseph	4th Ct. Militia	Root
Ives, Levi Dr.	Medical	Johnston, Rockwell
Jessup, Joseph	Wilton Militia	Hubbard, Pension Record
Johnson, Justus**	13th Ct. Militia	Hubbard
Jones, Eaton Capt.	Litchfield Militia	Seymour
Jones, Ebenezer	1st R-field Militia	Teller, Rockwell
Keeler, Jeremiah	Volunteer	Van Norden, Hurd, Keeler
		Family, Grumman
Keeler, Nehemiah	16th Ct. Militia	Keeler Family Records
Lamb, John Col.	2nd Cont. Artillery	Gates, Hadaway
Lemmon, George**	4th Ct. Militia	Johnston, Hubbard
Knapp, Sylvanus** Capt.	9th Ct. Militia	Johnston, Hubbard, Wicks &
		Olsen
Lawrence, Samuel Capt.	3rd Westchtr Mil.	Rockwell, Van Norden, NY
		State Militia Roster
Lawrence, ? (Son of above)		Van Norden, Rockwell
Lockwood, James Sgt.	4th Westchtr Mil.	Holden & Lockwood
Lloyd, Clement Sgt.	5th Ct. Line	Wicks & Olsen, U.S. Army
		Records
Marvin, Ozias Capt.	Norwalk Militia	Marvin & Marvin,
		Danenberg, Johnston
Mather, Simeon	Woodbury	Grumman, Cothren
Mather, Timothy	Woodbury	Grumman, Cothren
Mead, John Col.	9th Ct. Militia	Johnston, Wicks & Olsen,
		Mead
Mead, Lebbeus	3rd New York Line	Van Norden, Grumman
Mead, Theophilius**	Wilton Militia	Hubbard, Pension records
Mosely, Increase Col.	13th Ct. Militia	Woodbury '76 Bicentennial
		Cothren, Johnston
Middlebrook, Ephraim* Lt.	4th Ct. Militia	Beach, Johnston
Nichols, Ebenezer	16th Ct, Militia	Rockwell
Nichols, Jesse		Hubbard
Nickerson, Jonathan	Quartermasters	Pension records
Noble, William	16th Ct. Militia	Rockwell
Northrop, Benjamin		Johnston, Welsh
Northrop, James		Johnston, Bedini
Olmstead, David Capt.		Bedini
Olmstead, Jesse	Wilton Militia	Hubbard
Olmstead, Stephen	1st Rfield Militia	Rockwell

Parmalee, Thomas**	Sgt.	Unnamed Militia	Clark
Patchen, David		4th Ct. Militia	Lathrop
Patchen, Ebenezer		5th Ct. Line	Case, Grumman, Todd
Phillips, Reuben		16th Ct. Militia	Rockwell
Read, Zalmon,	Capt.	4th Ct. Militia	Grumman
Richards, Isaac**		9th Ct. Militia	Hubbard, Johnston, Wicks & Olsen, Clark, Bayles
Ruggles, Joseph Jr.	Capt.	Brookfield Militia	Hawley
Sanford, David			Todd, Grumman
Scott, Moses		Wilton Militia	Hubbard
Seeley, Samuel*		4th Ct. Militia	Rockwell, Hurd
Selleck, David*		Volunteer	Lewisboro Book Committee, Wicks & Olsen
Seymour, Samuel	Capt.	Litchfield Militia	Seymour
Smith, Abraham*			Rockwell
Smith, Benjamin	Lt.	5th Ct. Line	Rockwell, Betz, U.S. Army Records
Smith, Elijah		1st R-field Militia	Rockwell
Smith, John			Johnston
Sterling, Thaddeus		Wilton Militia	Hubbard, Pension record
Stevens, David*		9th Ct. Militia	Rockwell, Huntington, Wicks & Olsen
Stevens, Peter		9th Ct. Militia	Wicks & Olsen
Terrell, John		16th Ct. Militia	Rockwell
Thompson, William*	Lt.	4th Ct. Militia	Sheftall, Johnston, Howe
Tomlinson, Beach			Rockwell, Grumman
Torrance, Thomas**		13th Ct. Militia	Cothren, Grumman
Travis, Jonathan**			Wicks & Olsen
Waterbury, David		9th Ct. Militia	Rockwell, Grumman
Waterbury, Isaac			Rockwell
Waterbury, John Jr.**		9th Ct. Militia	Hubbard, Johnston
Waterbury, Samuel			Wicks & Olsen
Weed, Ananias			Wicks & Olsen
Weed, Benjamin**		9th Ct. Militia	Grumman, Wicks & Olsen
Weed, Jabez			Wicks & Olsen
Weed, Smith**			Wicks & Olsen
Wells, Stephen**	Lt.	4th Ct. Militia	Hubbard, Grumman
Whiting, Samuel**	Col.	4th Ct. Militia	Debany, Howe

Summary of Sources Listed Above

Bailey, James Montgomery. *History of Danbury, Conn. 1684-1896; Compiled with Additions by Susan Benedict Hill,* New York: Burr, 1896.

Bayles, Lois. "Canaan Parish and the American Revolution," New Canaan Historical Society 1976 Annual Report, vol.VII, no. 2.

Bedini, Silviio, *Ridgefield in Review,* New Haven: The Walker-Rackliff Company, 1958.

Betz, F. Lee. "Ridgefield's Continentals, Men of the 5th Connecticut Regiment," An Eleven Page monograph in the possession of the Keeler Tavern Preservation Society, dated 16 March 1986.

Case, James R. *An Account of Tryon's Raid on Danbury and the Battle of Ridgefield*, Danbury: Danbury Printing Company for the Author, 1927.

Caulkins, Frances M. *History of Norwich, CT.*, Norwich: Published for the Author, 1866.

Clark, Murtie June. *The Pension Lists of 1792-95: with other Revolutionary War Pension Records*, Published for the Author, 1991.

Collections of the Connecticut Historical Society, Vol. 12, Hartford: Case, Lockwood & Brainard, 1909.

Connecticut Historical Society Collections, Vol. 8, Revolution Lists and Rolls, p. 60 & p. 152

Cothren, William. *History of Ancient Woodbury, Conn.*, Waterbury: William R. Seeley, 1871.

Debany, Walter H. *The Connecticut Militia 1775-1783*. Norwalk: Home Press, 1992.

Grumman, William E., *The Revolutionary Soldiers of Redding*, Hartford: Case, Lockwood & Brainard, 1904.

Hadaway, William S., Editor, *The McDonald Papers*, White Plains: The Westchester County Historical Society, 1927.

Hawley, Emily. *Annals of Brookfield; Fairfield County, Connecticut*, Brattleboro: E. Hildreth & Co., 1929.

Holden, Frederic A., and Lockwood, E. Dunbar. *Colonial and Revolutionary History of the Lockwood Family in America*, Philadelphia: For the Authors, 1889.

Howe, Sir William, *Letter from the Hon. General Sir William Howe to Lord Geo. Germain, dated New York, April 24, 1777, received by the* Mercury, Packet, as published in the *London Gazette* on June 5, 1777.

Hubbard, G. Evans, *Wilton Village: A History*, An Unpublished Manuscript in the Possession of the Wilton Historical Society Collection, Version One, Part Two, 1936.

Letter from Colonel Hugh Hughes to General Horatio Gates, 3 May 1777, *Gates Papers*, in possession of The New York Historical Society.

Huntington, Reverend E. B., *History of Stamford*, Stamford: Wm. W. Gillespie & Co., 1868.

Hurd, D. Hamilton, *History of Fairfield County, Connecticut*, Philadelphia: J. W. Lewis & Co., 1881.

Johnston, Henry P., Editor. *The Record of Connecticut Men in the Military and Naval Service During the War of the Revolution 1775-1783*, Hartford: Case Lockwood, Brainard Company, 1889.

Keeler, Wesley B., *Keeler Family*, Baltimore: Gateway Press, 1985.

Lathrop, Cornelia Penfield, *Black Rock, Seaport of Old Fairfield, CT. 1644-1870, Including the Wheeler Journal*, New Haven: Tuttle, Morehouse and Taylor, 1930.

Lewisboro Book Committee, *A History of the Town of Lewisboro*, South Salem, New York: For the authors, 1981.

Marvin, George F. & Marvin, William T. R.,   *The Marvin Family; Descendents of Reinold and Matthew 1635-1904,* Boston: T. R. Marvin & Son, 1904

McDonald, John M., 1100 pages of notes encompassing a personal history of the Revolutionary War in Westchester County, New York, comprised of 407 interviews with 207 persons aged 70-96 between 1844 and 1850. The papers are in the possession of the Westchester County Historical Society.

Office of the New York State Comptroller. *New York in the Revolution,* Albany: J. B. Lyon Company, 1904.

Orcutt, Reverend Samuel, *History of Stratford and Bridgeport, Conn. 1639-1886,* New Haven: Tuttle, Morehouse and Taylor, 1886.

Revolutionary War Pension Applications, National Archives Record Group 15 of the Records of the Veterans Administration.

Robertson, Archibald. *His Diaries and Sketches in America 1762-1780,* New York: The New York Public Library, 1880.

Rockwell, George   Lounsbury.   *A History of Ridgefield, Connecticut,* reprinted from the original edition privately printed by the author in 1927, New York: Harbor Hill Books, 1979.

Root, Mary   Philotheta, Editor. Chapter Sketches,   *CT Daughters of the American Revolution: Patriots Daughters,* New Haven: Edward P. Judd Co., 1904.

Schonnard, Frederick, and Spooner. W. N., *History of Westchester County,* Harrison, New York: Harbor Hill Books, 1914.

Seymour, George D. &   Jacobus, Donald L.   *A History of the Seymour Family,* New Haven: Tuttle, Morehouse & Taylor, 1939.

Sheftall, John McKay. *The Dimons of Fairfield CT, A Family History,* Roswell, Georgia: W. H. Wolfe Associates, 1983.

Teller, Daniel. *The History of Ridgefield,* Danbury: T. Donovan, 1878.

Todd, Charles Burr.   *The History of Redding, Connecticut,* New York: Grafton Press, 1906,

U.S. Army Center of Military History, Organizational Research Branch, 1099 14th St. NW, Washington D.C., *Fifth Connecticut Line: Formation of 1777-1781.*

Van   Norden, Theodore Langdon.   *South Salem Soldiers and Sailors,* Lancaster, PA: Lancaster Press, 1927.

Wicks, Edith M., and   Olsen,Virgina. *Stamford's Soldiers; Genealogical Biographies of Revolutionary War Veterans from Stamford, CT.,* Stamford: Ferguson Library, 1976.

Wilcoxson, William H. *History of Stratford, CT,* Bridgeport: Brewer-Borg Corporation, 1940.

Appendix C

The following comprehensive report of the losses suffered by the inhabitants of Ridgefield during Tryon's raid, was submitted to the Connecticut General Assembly 5 December 1777 by the Committee appointed to investigate sufferer claims. (Revolutionary War Manuscript Collection, Connecticut State Archives, Hartford)

To the Hon^{bl} General Assembly of ye State of Connecticut to be holden at Hartford by adjournment on ye 2nd Thursday of January 1778. — We the Subscribers a Comm^{tte} appointed by Your Hon^{rs} at your Session in May last upon the Memorial of the Select Men of the Town of Ridgefield, Representing that the Enemy in their Late Incursion to Danbury on their Return passed thro said Ridgefield and burned many Dwelling houses as other Buildings therein, Killed and carried off many of their Cattle, and plundered the inhabitants of their Provision, and much of their Clothing.—

And we being appointed Com^{tte} as afors^d to estimate the losses of every Individual in said Town of Ridgefield in consequence of said Hostilities and Report make to this or some future Assembly so that ye Real losses the unhappy Sufferers have sustained by the Desolation and Ravage of our Merciless Enemies may thereby be clearly known, and such Representation made thereof and attention to the Condition of the Unfortunate as any future Assembly may think proper, etc.—

We beg leave to Report that in pursuance of s^d Commission we Repaired to said Ridgefield on ye 1st day of December (having first notified the Inhabitants) and by several adjournments down to this day we have examined the Acct^s of the several sufferers on Oath and otherwise according to the best of our Discretion and fixed that ye several Persons hereafter Named have suffered loss to the amount of the sum affixed to their names —

Sam^{ll} Olmstead Eqr.	112- 8- 1	Gamaliel Northrop	131-10- 4
Ebenez^r Olmsted	9- 2	Benjm Northrop	239- 1
Thad^{us} Rockwell	40- 7	Danl Smith	274-16- 8
Saml Olmsted 3	35-10- 4	John Northrop	214- 5-11
Col. Philip B. Bradley	30-14	Thoms Saymor	98-14- 9
Lydia Gilbard	51-15- 9	Hannah Saymor	27-10-10
Timothy Keeler	78-14- 0	Sarah Morehouse	284- 1- 9
	£358-11- 2		£1270- 1- 3
Capt. David Olmsted	54- 3-	Revn Saml Camp	58- 6- 9
Joseph Stebbins	29-14-	Isaac Keeler	291- 0
Dan^{ll} Smith	46- 9- 9	Lemuel Abot	8-14
James Sturgis	15-17- 6	James Northrop	80-16
John Dauchy	16-16	Abraham Rockwell	16- 1-16
George Follit	19- 6	John Keeler	48- 0- 6
Dan^{ll} Smith Jr	4- 0	Capt. Timothy Benedict	10- 7- 9
Capt. Ebenezer Jones	7-17	Capt. Ichabod Doolittle	8-13- 0
Bartlet Follit	8- 6- 3	Jarminda Keeler	1- 8- 0
Ebenez^r Stebbins	2-19- 6	David Rockwell	12- 6- 9
Jeff Benedict	17- 5- 3	Sam^{ll} Keeler	6-19- 6
John Abot	6- 4- 0	Ebenez^r Sherwood	7-15- 0
Bartholomew Weed	5-10- 0	Stephⁿ Norris	4-10- 0
Hope Rhodes	11- 5- 0	Dan^{ll} Cooley Esq.	2-18- 0
Stephⁿ Smith	12- 7- 6	Mary Hays	5-14- 0
Martha Keeler	6- 3- 6	Abijah Rockwell	4-17- 9
John Waters	5- 8- 0	Abijah Smith	25- 1- 0
David Perry	4-13-0	Jona Foster	16-17- 3
Capt. James Scott	3-19-0	Sarah Silster	4- 0- 6
Phillip Dauchy	5- 2- 6	Elihu DeForest	3
Matthew Keeler	10- 5- 0	Prne Northrop	6- 0- 6
John Smith	20- 0- 9	Nathan Foster	0-16- 0
Sam^{ll} Smith	28- 2- 9	Mary Gray	2
Benj^{mn} Smith	7- 1- 0	David Rockwell Jr.	4-14- 3
Jeremiah Burchard	0-18- 0	Abner Wilson	13-10- 0
	£349-14-3	Samuel Keeler Jr.	2- 1- 6
			£646-15-0
			349-14-3
			358-11-2
			1270- 1-3
			£2625-1-8

Amounting in the whole to L2625-1-8 all
Which is Humbly Submitted to your Hon^{rs} by your
Hon^{rs} most Obedient humble Serv^{ts}

Ridgefield ye 5th Decem^r
AD 1777—

Appendix D

By Commodore Sir GEORGE COLLIER, Commander In Chief of His MAJESTY'S Ships and Veffels in North America; and Major-General WILLIAM TRYON, Commanding His MAJESTY'S Land Forces on a Separate Expedition.

A D D R E S S,
To the Inhabitants of CONNECTICUT.

The ungenerous and wanton Infurrection againft the Sovereignty of GREAT BRITAIN, into which this Colony, has been deluded by the Artifices of desperate and defigning Men, for private Purpofes, might well justify in you every Fear, which confcious Guilt could form refpecting the Intentions of the present Armament.

Your Towns, your Property, yourselves, lie ftill within the graft of that Power, whofe Forbearance you have ungeneroufly conftrued into Fear; but whofe Lenity has Pefifted in its mild and noble Efforsts, even though branded with the most unworthy Imputation.

The Exiftence of a fingle Habitation on your defencelefs Coaft, ought to be a conftant Reproof to your Ingratitude. Can the Strength of your whole Province cope with the Force which might at any Time be poured through every Destination in your Country? ———— You are confcious it cannot. Why then will you perfift in a ruinous and ill-judged Refiftance?

We have hoped that you would recover from the Phrenzy, which has diftracted this un-happy Country; and we believe the Day to be now come, when the greater part of this Continent begin to blufh at their Delusion. You, who lie fo much in our Power, afford the moft striking Monument of our Mercy, and therefore ought to fet the first example of returning to Allegiance.

Reflect upon what Gratitude requires of you; if that is infufficent to move you, attend to your own Inter15ft: We offer you a Refuge against the Distrefs, which you univerfally acknowledge, broods with increafing and intolerable Weight over all your Country.

Leaving you to confult with each other upon this Invitation ; We do now delclare, ———— That whofoever fhall be found, and remain in Peace, at his ufual Place of Refidence, fhall be fhielded from any Infult, either to his Perfon, or his Property; excepting fuch as bear Offices either Civil or Military, under your prefent ufurped Government : Of whom, it will be further required, that they fhall gove Proofs of ther Penitence abd voluntary Submiffion; and they fhall then partake the like Immunity.

Thofe, whofe Folly and Obftinacy may flight this favorable Warning, muft take Notice ; that they are not to expect a Continuance of that Lenity, which their Inveteracy would now render blameable.

GIVEN on Board His MAJESTY'S Ship CAMILLA,
In the Sound, July 4th, 1779.

GEORGE COLLIER,
WM. TRYON

* *

New-York : Printed by Macdonald & Cameron

George Washington Papers at the Library of Congress, 1741-1799: Series 4. General Correspondence 1697-1799, Images 1034 & 1035.

Appendix E

Glenna Welsh began the excruciating task of documenting Ridgefield's original Town Street residences in her 1976 work, *The Proprietors of Ridgefield.* After pinpointing locations for the first five of twenty-eight original proprietor lots, Welsh invited those who followed to complete the project. Having accepted her challenge, this piece offers the first complete picture (*Figure Three* on page 16) of property ownership as it had evolved by the Battle of Ridgefield. Like Welsh's pioneering work, this effort, too, must be considered a work in progress, upon which later students of history are invited to improve.

The original proprietors first laid out the town in a thoroughly logical fashion along Town Street. Beginning with Lot 1 at the southeastern end, twelve lots were laid out in ascending northward order on the eastern side of Town Street. Lot 13 was then placed across the street to the west, slightly to the south and opposite of Lot 12. Lots 14 through 26 continued southward in ascending order (lot 26 at the bottom), all bounded easterly by Town Street. Lots 27 and 28 (with Town Street in between) were then assigned respectively to the north of Lots 12 and 13.

So far, so good, but the plot soon thickened: Joseph Crampton (Lot 22) found his property unsatisfactory, and was given a replacement lot to the south of Lot 26. What's more, Lots 23, 24, & 25 turned out to be undersized when bog land was taken into account, and all three proprietors were given an additional acre-and-a-half directly across Town Street below Lot 1. Well, *almost* directly across Town Street. It seems that one early pioneer staked his claim prior to formal division of the first 28 lots in 1712. Back in 1710, Joseph Whitne had sized his home lot on the ground just below Lot 1; therefore the three compensatory lots lay directly south of Whitne's property.

By 1717, tanner Benjamin Stebbins and miller Daniel Sherwood were lured to Ridgefield with real estate grants along Town Street to the north of Lots 27 and 28 respectively. At this point all semblance of order stopped as a wave of new settlers purchased surrounding common land from the proprietors in no particular order or pattern.

What follows below is the provenance of each dwelling that appears on *Figure Three*, "Ridgefield Village, April 1777." The documentation begins with Joseph Whitne's plot located below Lot 1, and continues in the above-described sequence through all twenty-eight original lots. All later dwellings are listed in chronological order up to the year 1777. Each listing details the year of every property ownership transfer, each new owner's name, and the volume/page where the transaction may be found in Ridgefield Land Records. To the best of my knowledge, the final name on each house record was the owner (not necessarily the inhabitant) in 1777.

Prior to formal 1712 Division: Joseph Whitne
>   **Location:** East side of Town Street, below Lot 1.
>   **Ownership record:**
>>   1713: Richard Whitne   RLR: 1/40
>>   1713: Richard Osborne   RLR: 1/41
>>   1743: Jeremiah Osborne   RLR: 3/120
>>   1762: Benjamin Keeler   RLR: 4/217
>>   1762: James Sturges RLR: 4/224

Lot 1. Original Proprietor: 1712, Samuel St. John
>   **Location:** North of Joseph Whitne, east of Town Street.
>   **Ownership record:**
>>   1729: Lemuel Morehouse   RLR: 2/72
>>   1739: Daniel Chapman   RLR: 3/2
>>   1745: Albert Chapman   RLR: 3/150
>>   1746: Lt. Benjamin Hoyt   RLR: 3/176
>>   1759: Benjamin Hoyt Jr.   Danbury Probate Court
>>   Records: 1/155

Lot 2. Original Proprietor: 1710, Samuel Keeler Sr.
> **Location:** North of Samuel St. John, south of Jonathan
> Rockwell, east of Town Street.
>
> **Ownership record:**
>> 1710: Samuel Keeler Jr. RLR: 1/27
>> 1711: Jonathan Rockwell RLR: 1/26
>> 1712: Daniel Hoyt RLR: 1/39
>> 1713: Benjamin Hoyt RLR: 1/43
>> 1759: David Hoyt Danbury Probate Records, 1/155
>> 1769: Timothy Keeler Jr. RLR: 5/77

Lot 3. Original Proprietor: 1712, Jonathan Rockwell
> **Location:** North of Samuel Keeler Sr., south of Thomas
> Canfield, east of Town Street. Just below southeast
> corner of meeting yard according to old Whitne
> Bible inscription.
>
> **Ownership record:**
>> 1733: Jonathan, Benj.& David Rockwell RLR: 2/156
>> 1747: John Gilbert RLR: 3/305
>> 1753: Josiah Gilbert RLR: 4.41
>> 1767: Benjamin Keeler RLR: 5/27
>> 1768: Jeremiah Keeler RLR: 5/64

Lot 4. OriginalProprietor: 1708, Thomas Canfield
> **Location:** North of Jonathan Rockwell, south of highway,
> east of Town Street.
>
> **Ownership Record:**
>> 1709: Henry Whitne RLR: 1/34
>> 1745: **Subdivided**
>> South Half: John Whitne RLR: 3/156
>>> 1753: Abraham Betts RLR: 4/41
>> North Half: Daniel Whitne RLR: 3/156
>>> 1752: Gideon Betts RLR: 4/31
>>> 1754: Elijah Hawley RLR: 4/81
>>> 1756: Darius Lobdell RLR: 4/116
>>> 1756: John Olmstead RLR: 4/125
>>> 1758: Jacob Jones RLR: 4/218
>>> 1763: Samuel & Sarah Lobdell RLR: 4/235
>>> 1775: Benjamin Darling RLR: 5/245

Lot 5. Reserve for Original Minister: Reverend Thomas Hauley
> **Location:** North of highway, south of Matthias St. John, east

of Town Street, west of highway
Ownership Record:
      1714: Reverend Thomas Hauley   RLR: 1/45
      1738: Elijah Hauley   Danbury Probate Records
      1767: Elizabeth Hauley   RLR: 5/25

Lot 6. Original Proprietor: 1712, Matthias St. John
    Location: North of Proprietor Reserve, south of Joseph
                Whitne, east of Town Street, west of highway
    Ownership Record:
      1717: Nathan St. John   RLR: 1/83
      1749: Hannah St. John   Danbury Probate Records
      1753: Nathan St. John Jr.   RLR: 4/44
      1753: Matthew Seamore   RLR: 4/66
      1756: Josiah Gilbert Jr.   RLR: 4/120
      1762: Thaddeus Sturges   RLR: 4/214

Lot 7. Original Proprietor: 1712, Joseph Whitne
    Location: North of Matthias St. John, south of highway, east
                of Town Street, west of highway
    Ownership Record:
      1713: Richard Whitne   RLR: 1/40
      1713: Richard Osborne   RLR: 1/41
      1728: Benjamin Wilson   RLR: 2/60
      1739: Benjamin Wilson Jr.   RLR: 3/76
      1759: Deborah Wilson, three sons & four daughters
             Danbury Probate Records 5/250

Lot 8. Original Proprietor: 1712, Milford Samuel Smith
    Location: North of highway, south of James Brown, east of
                Town Street, west of highway
    Ownership Record:
      1749: 1/2 to Jacob Smith   RLR: 3/256
      1764: Remainder to Jacob Smith, Danbury Probate
             Records 2/179-183

Lot 9. Original Proprietor: 1712, James Brown
    Location:
        South of John Belden, north of Samuel Smith, east of
        Town Street, west of highway.
    Ownership Record:
      1713: **Subdivided**

North Half: Joshua Lobdell   RLR: 1/39
   1742: Caleb Lobdell   RLR: 3/73
South Half: Joseph Tompkins   RLR: 1/42
   1713: John Copp   RLR: 1/42
   1714: Moses Northrop   RLR: 1/72
   1716: Joshua Lobdell   RLR: 1/106
   1742: Darius Lobdell   RLR: 3/87
   1759: Matthew Seamor   RLR: 4/153
   1763: William Carpenter   RLR: 4/253
   1765: Nathan Hubbell   RLR: 5/18
   1771: Samuel Carpenter   RLR: 5/133
   1773: Jeremiah Wilson   RLR: 5/158

Lot 10. Original Proprietor: 1712, John Belden
   Location: South of R. Olmstead, north of James Brown, east
      of Town Street, west of highway
   Ownership Record:
      1713: Benjamin Benedict   RLR: 1/43
      1750: Timothy Benedict   RLR: 3/273
      1775: Bartlet Foliot   RLR: 5/248

Lot 11. Original Proprietor: 1712, Richard Olmstead
   Location: South of Thomas Smith, north of John Belden, east
      of Town Street, west of highway
   Ownership Record
      North Lot (1/2 acre)
         1760: Daniel Olmstead   RLR: 4/183
         1765: Epenetus How   RLR: 4/266
         1771: John Watrous   RLR: 5/132
      South Lot
         1765: Samuel Olmstead Jr.   RLR: 5/121
         1765: Josiah Stebbins RLR: 5/124

Lot 12. Original Proprietor: 1712, Thomas Smith
   Location: South of Highway, north of Richard Olmstead, east
      of Town Street, west of highway
   Ownership Record:
      1744: David Smith   RLR: 3/124
      1752: Isaac & Thomas Smith   RLR: 4/29

Lot 13. Original Proprietor: 1712, Jonathan Stevens
   Location: North of Thomas Sturdivant, south of highway,

west of Town Street, east of highway
Ownership Record:
    1712: Mary Bouton
    1712: David Scott RLR: 1/47
    1741: Vivus Dauchy   RLR: 3/215

Lot 14. Original Proprietor: 1712, John Sturdivant
    Location: North of Thomas Hyatt, west of Town Street, east
        of highway
    Ownership Record:
        West Section (Two acres)
            1715: Joseph Platt RLR: 1/46
            1715: Thomas Hyatt RLR: 1/47
            1759: Thomas Hyatt Jr., Danbury Probate Records
                1/175-76
            1772: Hannah Hyatt / Samuel Smith RLR: 5/174
        East Section (5 1/2 acres)
            1731: John Sturdivant Jr, Samuel, Elizabeth and
                Bula (Fairfield Probate Record)

Lot 15. Original Proprietor: 1712,Thomas Hyatt
    Location: North of Benjamin Wilson, south of John
        Sturdivant, west of Town Street, east of highway
    Ownership Record:
        1759: Thomas Hyatt Jr. Danbury Probate Records
            1/175-76
        1772: Hannah Hyatt / Samuel Smith RLR: 5/174

Lot 16. Original Proprietor: 1712, Benjamin Wilson
    Location: South of Thomas Hyatt, west of Town Street, east
        of highway, north of Benj. Hitchcock
    Ownership Record:
        1742: Nathan Wilson
        1762: Benjamin Rockwell RLR 4/270
        1767: Nathan Wilson RLR: 5/32
        1771: Ezekiel Wilson RLR: 5/126

Lot 17. Original Proprietor: 1712, Benjamin Hitchcock
    Location: North of Matthew St John, south of Benjamin
        Wilson, west of Town Street, east of highway
    Ownership Record:
        1711: Thomas Rockwell RLR: 1/37

1732: John & Jabez Rockwell   RLR: 2/178
1736: Jabez Rockwell   RLR: 2/162
1739: Peter Burr   RLR: 3/5
1739: Reverend Jonathan Ingersoll   RLR: 3/51

Lot 18. Original Proprietor: 1712, Matthew St. John
    Location: North of Joseph Keeler, south of Benjamin
         Hitchcock, west of Town Street, east of highway
    Ownership Record:
         1723: Joseph Lees   RLR: 1/70
         1737: Peter Burr   RLR: 2/195
         1742: Elijah Hauley   RLR: 3/80
         1750: Samuel Smith 3rd RLR: 3/275
         1774: Lt. Benjamin Smith   RLR: 6/24

Lot 19. Original Proprietor: 1712, Joseph Keeler
    Location: South of Matthew St. John, north of Matthew
         Seamor, west of Town Street, east of highway
    Ownership Record:
         1744: Lott Keeler   RLR: 3/141
         1749: Silas Keeler   RLR: 3/192
         1758: Silas Baldwin   RLR: 4/141
         1760: Ephraim Jackson   RLR: 4/167
         1761: Nathan Wilson   RLR: 4/207
         1761: Dr. John Andreas Jr.   RLR: 4/210

Lot 20. Original Proprietor: 1712, Matthew Seamor
    Location: North of James Benedict, south of Joseph Keeler,
         west of Town Street, east of highway
    Ownership Record:
         1716: Matthew Seamor Junior   RLR: 1/50
         1721: James Benedict   RLR: 1/191
         1755: Peter Benedict   RLR: 4/97
         1765: Gideon Smith & Thomas Rockwell   RLR: 5/24
         1770: John Andreas, Jr.   RLR: 5/96

Lot 21. Original Proprietor: 1712, James Benedict
    Location: North of Joseph Crampton, south of Matthew
         Seamor, west of Town Street, east of highway
    Ownership Record:
         1765: Peter, John, Thomas, James, Sarah (Smith),
            Ruth (Rockwell), and Martha (Scott) Benedict

RLR: 4/273.

1770: John Andreas Jr., 2nd dwelling retained by
John Benedict RLR: 5/96

1773: one acre w/ original dwelling to David
Olmstead RLR: 5/214

Lot 22. Original Proprietor: 1712, Joseph Crampton
    Location: North of highway & common land, west of
        highway and east of common land.
    Ownership Record:
        1720: Jonathan Abbott RLR 1/149
        1720: Jonathan Abbott Jr. RLR: 1/150
        Northwest Lot:
            1726: Timothy Canfield RLR: 2/40
            1729: Gamaliel Northrop RLR: 2/46
            1729: John Northrop   RLR: 2/72
            1775: Josiah Hine   RLR: 5/244
        Northeast Lot:
            1728: Jonathan Abbott RLR: 2/64
            1745: Jonathan Abbott Jr. RLR: 3/174
            1763: Isaac Keeler by mortgage from Michael
                Abbott RLR: 6/146
        South Lot:
            1728: Jonathan Abbott Jr. RLR: 2/70
            1745: Matthew Benedict RLR: 3/178
            1768: Jesse Benedict RLR: 5/40, 5/41, & 5/221
        West Lot:
            1728: Lemuel Abbott   RLR: 2/55
            1760: John Osborn RLR: 4/190
            1763: Michael & Jonathan Abbott   RLR: 5/87
            1770: Benjamin Hoyt   RLR: 5/86

Lot 23. Original Proprietor: 1712, Norwalk Samuel Smith
    Location: Bounded south by Daniel Olmstead, east by Town
        Street, north by highway & common land, west by
        common land
    Ownership Record:
        1764: Samuel Smith Jr. RLR: 4/254

Lot 24. Original Proprietor: 1712, Daniel Olmstead
    Location: North of Samuel Keeler Sons, south of Samuel
        Smith, west of Town Street, east of pasture of

Daniel Olmstead
Ownership Record:
  1728: Gamaliel Northrop   RLR: 2/66
  1770: James Scott   RLR: 5/89
  1773: David Olmstead   RLR: 5/214

Lot 25. Original Proprietor: 1710, Samuel Keeler Sr.
  Location: Bounded north and west by Daniel Olmstead, south
    by Joseph Benedict, east by Town Street.
  Ownership Record:
    1710: Samuel Keeler Sr.   RLR: 1/27
    1717: Timothy Keeler   RLR: 1/87
    1749: Benjamin Keeler   Danbury Probate Records
      2/17
    1773: Martha Keeler and Benjamin Keeler Jr.
      Danbury Probate Records 5/418

Lot 26. Original Proprietor: 1712, Joseph Benedict
  Location: Bordered north by Samuel Keeler Jr., south by
    Joseph Crampton, east by Town Street and west by
    Common land
  Ownership Record:
    West Lot:
      1714: James Northrop   RLR: 1/53
      1762: Benjamin Northrop and James Northrop Jr.
    East Lot: (Divided in half)
      1731: Timothy Keeler   RLR: 2/119 (home lot
        bounded north by Keeler, south by Abbott,
        east by Town Street and west by Joseph
        Benedict
      1731: Benjamin Hoyt   RLR: 2/220 (Bounded
        west by highway, north by James and
        Gamaliel Northrop, south by Abbott, and
        John Northrop, east by Timothy Keeler)

Lot 27. Original Proprietor: 1712, Ebenezer Smith
  Location: Bordered south and west by highway, north by
    pasture and east by common.
  Ownership Record:
    1744: Ebenezer Smith Jr. Danbury Probate Records
    1756: Northern Half to Ebenezer Smith (3rd)
      Southern Half to John Smith

Lot 28. Original Proprietors to: Benjamin Burt, 1712
>> **Location:** Bounded north by Daniel Sherwood, south and
>> west by highways and east by Town Street.
>> **Ownership Record:**
>> 1780: Absconded to British, Land seized

Proprietors Common Land: to Benjamin Stebbins, 1717
>> **Location:** Bounded North by Steep Brook, south common
>> land, west by highway, east by common land
>> **Ownership Record**
>> 1717: Benjamin Stebbins   RLR: 1/69

Proprietors Common Land: to Daniel Sherwood, 1717
>> **Location:** Bounded west by Town Street, south by Benjamin
>> Burt, north by common land and James Wallis
>> **Ownership Record:**
>> 1717: Daniel Sherwood   RLR: 1/62
>> 1770: Mary Sherwood (Danbury Probate Records)
>> 1773: John Sherwood   RLR: 5/19

Other Documented In town Dwellings

Philip Burr Bradley House
>> **Location:** North, east and west by highway, south by John
>> Sherwood.
>> **Ownership Record:**
>> 1764: Philip Burr Bradley   RLR: 4/253

Jeremiah Keeler House
>> **Location:** Bounded west by Town Street, south by Jeremiah
>> and Jonah Keeler and north by Samuel Smith
>> **Ownership Record:**
>> 1768: Jeremiah Keeler   RLR: 5/65

Ezekiel Olmstead House
>> **Location:** Bounded west by Town Street, south by Jeremiah
>> and Jonah Keeler
>> **Ownership Record:**
>> 1752: Daniel Olmstead   RLR: 4/25
>> North Lot:
>> 1754: Jonathan Olmstead   RLR: 4/69

1754: leased to Daniel Olmstead   RLR: 4/79
1758: Heirs of Jonathan Olmstead
South Lot:
    1752: Ezekiel Olmstead   RLR: 4/27
    1753: Noah St. John   RLR: 4/59
    1756: Jeremiah Keeler   RLR: 4/113

Benjamin Rockwell House (circa 1740)
    Location: Westerly of Town Sreet, bounded east and north by highway, south by John Northrop.
    Ownership Record:
        1753: John Bouton   RLR: 4/70
        1754: Nathan Betts   RLR: 4/83
        1755: John Northrop Jr.   RLR: 4/100

Captain David Olmstead House (circa 1750)
    Location: Westerly of highway, south of John Rockwell Jr.
    Ownership Record: Bicentennial Landmark Committee map of 1976

Stephen Olmstead House (circa 1740)
    Location: Westerly of highway, south of David Olmstead
    Ownership Record: Bicentennial Landmark Committee map of 1976

Ensign James Benedict house (circa 1730)
    Location: Northerly of highway, easterly of James Sturges
    Ownership Record: Bicentennial Landmark Committee map of 1976

J. Benedict House (circa 1760)
    Location: East and south of highways
    Ownership Record: Bicentennial Landmark Committee map of 1976

X. Endnotes

I. Prologue

[1] After turning traitor in 1780 and taking command of a British force in Virginia, Benedict Arnold was ordered to quickly abandon his position in Richmond and proceed to Westover. Refusing a request from one of his officers to delay the march, Arnold allegedly cited British General William Tryon's experience at Ridgefield, remarking: "If General Tryon had marched from Danbury two hours sooner, he would have met with no opposition. Had he remained six hours later, his forces would never have regained their shipping." *The McDonald Papers*, edited by William S. Hadaway for The Westchester County Historical Society, 1926, Volume II, p. 127.

[2] Every comprehensive account of the American Revolution makes passing reference to the Ridgefield action. The earliest version to explore the incident in any detail was The Reverend James Murray's two-volume collection that first appeared in 1778: *An Impartial History of the War in America; From its Commencement, to the present time; Together With the Charters of the several COLONIES, and other Authentic Information. Likewise, The Rise, Progress, and Political Springs of the War now carrying-on between Great Britain and the United Powers of France, Spain, Holland, and America; With a particular Account of the several Engagements both by Sea and Land,* (Newcastle upon Tyne: Robson, 1778, Volume II). Other early accounts include a) William Gordon, *The History of the Origin, Rise, Progress and Establishment of the Independence of the United States* (London, for the author, 1788), b) David Ramsay, *The History of the American Revolution* (Philadelphia: R. Aitken & Son, 1789) and, c) William Russell, *The History of America from its Discovery by Columbus to the Conclusion of the Late War, With an Appendix containing an Account of the Rise and Progress of the Present Unhappy Dispute* (London: Fielding & Walker, 1788. As noted by Silvio Bedini in his 1987 Connecticut Historical Society Bulletin piece, all of these works, and many more, may have heavily plagiarized *The National Register, for the year 1777 through 1779,* a documentary serial that ran in the English press. For both original and comprehensive reading, also consult Sir George Otto Trevelyan, *The American*

Revolution (London, 1792), and Charles Stedman, *History of the Origin, Progress, and Termination of the American War* (London, 1794, 2 Volumes). The Stedman work is particularly valued for containing perhaps the finest reprinted maps of the American Revolution.

[3] Barber, John Warner. *Connecticut Historical Collections.* A facsimile reprint originally published in 1836 by John W. Warner. Hanover, NH: University Press of New England, 1996. Hollister, Gideon H. *The History of Connecticut, From the First Settlement to the Colony to the Adoption of the Present Constitution, 3 vols.* New Haven: Durrie & Peck, 1855. Lossing, Benson J. *The Pictorial Field-Book of the Revolution; or Illustrations, By Pen and Pencil, of the History, Biography, Scenery, Relics, and Traditions of the War for Independence,* New York: Harper, 1860.

[4] Collier, Christopher. *The Literature of Connecticut History*, Volume Six in the "Connecticut Scholar" series. Middletown, CT: Connecticut Humanities Council, 1983. This reference volume, a thorough compilation of state history source literature arranged by subject, is the point of embarkation for any serious voyage into Connecticut's past. Collier not only summarizes publications by topic, but also offers crisp commentary on the relevance and scholarship of each work published before 1983.

II. Southwestern Connecticut in 1777

[1] For an incisive account of British and American strategic options in spring, 1777, see James Thomas Flexner's *George Washington in the American Revolution (1775-1783)*, (Boston: Little, Brown & Company, 1967), pp. 202-206.

[2] Letter from General George Washington to Connecticut Governor Jonathan Trumbull, as quoted in John Marshall's *The Life of George Washington, Commander in Chief of the American Forces, During the War which Established the Independence of his Country, and First President of the United States, compiled under the inspection of The Honorable Bushrod Washington, from original papers bequeathed to him by his deceased relative,* Second Edition, revised and corrected by the Author. Philadelphia: James Crissy, 1834, Vol. I. Note VIII. p. 24.

[3] Hoadley, Charles J. *Public Records of the State of Connecticut, Correspondence of the General Assembly and Council of Safety from October 1776 to February, 1778, inclusive.* Hartford: Case, Lockwood & Brainard Company, 1894, pp. 196, 200, & 362.

[4] Hastings, Hugh, Editor, *Public Papers of George Clinton, First Governor of New York,* Albany 1899-1914, Vol. IV, pp 361 & 362. Major Lyons wrote to Governor Clinton in December 1778: "People in this neighborhood of Westchester send cows, oxen, and horses to the British." Lyons's pro-American stance evidently did not sit well with these neighbors and shortly thereafter Lyons vacated his Bedford homestead for the protection of Connecticut. After Yorktown, Lyons retrieved his property, and then some, from Loyalist usurpers.

[5] Mackenzie, Frederick. *Diary of Frederick Mackenzie,* Cambridge: Harvard University Press, 1930. Vol. I, p. 40.

[6] Schonnard, Frederick, and Spooner, W. N. *History of Westchester County,* Harrison, New York: Harbor Hill Books, 1974. p. 41.

[7] Buel, Joy Day and Richard Jr. *The Way of Duty: A Woman and Her Family in Revolutionary America,* New York: W.W. Norton & Company, 1984. p. 246.

[8] Wilcoxson, William H. *History of Stratford, Connecticut.* Bridgeport: Brewer-Borg Corporation, 1940.

[9] C.J. Hoadley and J.H. Trumbull, "Public Records of the Colony of Connecticut", as reproduced by Thomas L. Purvis in *Almanacs of American Life, Revolutionary America,* (New York: Facts on File, 1995). pp. 144-147.

[10] Jeffrey Amherst, *The Journal of Jeffrey Amherst,* ed. J. Clarence Webster (Chicago, 1931), App. A-D, pp 327-30.

[11] Letter from Jared Ingersoll to Governor Thomas Fitch, February 11, 1765. *A Web of English History* by Marjie Bloy, *http://dspace.dial.pipex.com. Mbloy/c-eight/sadebate.htm.*

[12] For a fascinating insight on the activities of the New York Sons of Liberty during the decade preceding Revolution, see Chapters I-IV of Isaac Q. Leake's *Memoirs of the Life and Times of General John Lamb,* originally published in Albany 1857, reprinted in 1970 by Benchmark Publishing Company Inc. of Glendale, New York.

[13] Ingersoll, John. *The Ingersolls of New Hampshire,* Boston; Mudge & Sons, 1893, pp. 23-24.

[14] Ridgefield Town Meeting Records, 1746-1797, p. 48.

[15] Haight, Robert S. *St. Stephens Church, Ridgefield, Connecticut, Its History for 250 years 1725 – 1975.* p. 22.

[16] Ridgefield Town Meeting Records, 1746-1797, p. 49.

[17] Marshall, John. Vol. I, p. 127.

[18] Buel, p. 203.

[19] As quoted from a letter from John Adams to Abigail Adams in David McCullough's *John Adams* (New York: Simon & Schuster, 2001), p. 78.

[20] Van Tyne, Claude Halstead. *The Loyalists in the American Revolution,* New York: The Macmillan Company, 1902, p. 157.

[21] Smith, Paul H., "The American Loyalists: Notes on Their Organization and Strength," <u>William & Mary Quarterly</u>, 3rd Ser., 25 (1968), 258-77. Because history is usually written by the victors, the depth of Loyalist affection throughout the colonies (particularly in Connecticut) comes as a surprise to most Americans. In addition to Smith's piece, other well-researched works are: Ohio State University Professor W. H. Siebert's *The Refugee Loyalists of Connecticut,* (Ottawa: Royal Society of Canada, 1916), Series III, volume X; Oscar Zeichner's *Connecticut's Years of Controversy,* (Chapel Hill: University of North Carolina Press, 1949), and Stephen P. McGrath's "Connecticut's Tory Towns; The Loyalty Struggle in Newtown, Redding, and Ridgefield," <u>Connecticut Historical Society Bulletin #44</u>, July 1979, pp. 88-96.

[22] *Forwarding message from Major General David Wooster to General James Wadsworth attached to letter dated Friday, April 25 from Brigadier General*

Gold Selleck Silliman to Wooster, in the possession of the Fairfield Historical Society.
[23] Bakeless, John. *Turncoats, Traitors & Heroes; Espionage in the American Revolution*, New York: Da Capo Press, 1998 (reprint of the edition first published in New York in 1959). p. 162.
[24] Bakeless, p. 292-294. Heron's dirty little secret emerged in 1882 when Dr. Thomas Emmitt produced the Private Intelligence records of Sir Henry Clinton. Now in the New York Public Library these documents reveal Heron to have operated under the code name "Hiram-the spy."
[25] Mackenzie, Vol. II, p. 446.
[26] The papers of Charles Beach as quoted by Charles Burr Todd, *The History of Redding, CT.*, New York: The Grafton Press, 1906. p. 96.
[27] Letter to Reverend John Beach from the Selectmen of Redding dated 2/12/1778, as quoted by Glenna M. Walsh, *The Proprietors of Ridgefield*, Ridgefield: Caudatowa Press, 1976, pp. 140-141.

III. The British Arrive

[1] *Report from Brigadier General Benedict Arnold to Brigadier General Alexander McDougall at Redding, Connecticut, Saturday, 27 April 1777, 10:00 P.M.* The Papers of the Continental Congress 1774-1780, Letters of Washington, 152,vol. III, pp. 1-595. Case, James R. *An Account of Tryon's Raid on Danbury in April 1777, also The Battle of Ridgefield and The Career of Gen. David Wooster*, Danbury, Ct.: Danbury Printing, 1927, p. 9. More specific detail is provided by Captain Archibald Robertson's diary in which he notes that 250 men each from six regiments of foot, ten mounted dragoons, and unspecified number of artillerymen along with six field pieces, and 300 men of Governor Montfort Browne's Prince of Wales Loyal American Volunteers disembarked at Compo Point. *Archibald Robertson, His Diaries and Sketches in America 1767-1780.* New York: New York Public Library, 1930. p. 126.
[2] Letter from John Field to Brig. Gen. McDougall from John Field, dated Sunday 12 o'clock, April 27, 1777, as published in *The Pennsylvania Evening Post* of May 1, 1777 (Vol.III, Num.346), copy now in the collection of the Danbury Historical Society.
[3] Letter from John Campbell to Gen. McDougall, as published in *The Pennsylvania Evening Post* of Thursday, May 1, 1777 (Vol.III, Num.346), copy now in the collection of the Danbury Historical Society.
[4] Hollister, Gideon H. *The History of Connecticut, From the First Settlement of the Colony to the Adoption of the Present Constitution*, 3 vols., New Haven: Durrie & Peck, 1855. pp. 296-308.
[5] Bailey, James Montgomery. *History of Danbury, Conn. 1684-1896; Compiled with Additions by Susan Benedict Hill*, New York: Burr, 1896. p. 69.
[6] Written Orders of Major General William Tryon, aboard the H.M. S. Senegal, dated April 23rd, 1777 as reproduced in Case, pp. 9 & 10.
[7] For a detailed description of both British and Continental military organization, see *1777 The Year of the Hangman*, by John S. Pancake

((University of Alabama Press, 1975), Chapter Five "Arms & Men". As recorded in Major H. G. Purdon's *Memoirs of the Service of the 64ᵗʰ Regiment,"* three months prior to embarking on the Danbury expedition the 64ᵗʰ mustered 551 men. This return dated 1/8/1777 lists 1 lt. colonel, 1 major, 7 captains, 10 lieutenants, 4 ensigns, 28 sergeants, 17 drummers, and 483 privates.

[8] The Prince of Wales Loyal American Volunteers muster of April 21, 1777 included 34 officers, 30 sergeants, 11 drummers, and 520 rank and file as detailed in Colonel Montfort Browne's letter to Sir Guy Carleton (Headquarters Papers of the British Army in America, Great Britain Public Record Office, PRO 30/557602). Captain Archibald Robertson's period diary entry for April 25 noted "300 Provincials of Governor Brown's Corps." The unmistakable conclusion is that these were hand picked men, most likely those who hailed from towns along Tryon's planned route.

[9] McCusker, John J. *Alfred, the First Continental Flagship, 1775-1778,* Smithsonian Studies in History and Technology, no. 20 (Washington, 1973), p. 5

[10] Letter from Major General of Provincials Montfort Browne to Lord George Germain, dated May 31, 1777 as quoted from William Grumman's *The Revolutionary Soldiers of Redding, Connecticut and the Record of their Services.* Hartford: 1904. p.57.

[11] As quoted from *New York Historical Documents, Vol. VII, p. 736,* in Claude Halstead Van Tyne's *The Loyalists in the American Revolution* (New York: The Macmillan Company, 1902), p. 67.

[12] As quoted from Colonel Mark M. Boatner III's *The Encyclopedia of the American Revolution,* by Glenna Welsh, *The Proprietors of Ridgefield* (Ridgefield: Caudatowa Press, 1976) p.137. When Royal Governor of North Carolina, Tryon in May of 1771 deployed a thousand infantry to squash a disorganized and poorly armed band of citizens known as "The Regulators" for their revolt against illegal fees and excessive taxes collected by dishonest Crown appointees. Also see McDevitt, p. 14.

[13] Letter from the Reverend John Vardill to William Eden, April 11,1778, Stevens, *Facsimiles of Manuscripts,* 4:438, as quoted by Nelson, Paul David, *William Tryon and the Course of Empire,* (Chapel Hill: University of North Carolina Press, 1990), p. 1.

[14] Letter from General Gage to the Earl of Dartmouth, dated Boston, 16ᵗʰ January, 1776. Isaac Q. Leake, *The Life and Times of General John Lamb,* originally published Albany, 1857, reprinted by Benchmark Publishing Company Inc, Glendale, New York, in 1970. p. 373. Dartmouth, one of Tryon's many political contacts in London, was Chancellor of the Exchequer during the Ministry of Lord North and well positioned at the King's ear.

[15] Letter from William Tryon to William Knox, *Manuscripts of Knox,* Colonial Office Papers, 5/154 Private Miscellaneous Correspondence.

[16] Letter from Governor William Tryon to Colonial Secretary Lord George Germaine dated December 31, 1776. Force, Peter, ed., *American Archives* Fifth Series (Washington: 1848-53), vol. III, p. 9.

[17] Letter from Major General William Tryon to Colonial Secretary Lord George Germain dated May 2, 1777, Force, Peter, ed., *American Archives,* Fifth Series, (Washington: 1848-53), vol. III.

[18] Robertson, p. 129.

[19] Mackenzie, Frederick. *Diary of Frederick Mackenzie 1775-1781,* Cambridge, Massachusetts: Harvard University Press, 1930. p. 39. Mackenzie's diary is one of the most extensive accounts of the War in America compiled by a Crown officer. Frustratingly absent however, is the period from January through May, 1777 – during which his regiment, the 23rd Foot, participated in Tryon's Danbury raid. Still, Mackenzie's promotion path is illustrative of the typical junior officer: Lieutenant 1745, Captain 1775, Major 1780, and then finally purchase of a commission as Lt. Colonel of the 37th Foot in 1787. He lived on half-pay until 1794 when he raised and commanded the First Exeter Volunteers in response to fear of Napoleon's potential invasion of England.

[20] *Letter from Horace Walpole to Sir Horace Mann dated August 11, 1777,* as quoted by Richard M. Ketchum, *Saratoga: Turning Point of America's Revolutionary War,* (New York: Henry Holt & Co., 1997), p. 77. Proud, silent Sir William Howe felt no need to apologize for posterity-sake his rationale for taking the field slowly and handling the rebel populace with restraint, thereby leaving generations of historians free to speculate about his motives. Regiments of armchair generals have since used perfect hindsight to fault Howe's behavior militarily, some going so far as to lay blame for America's victory at his feet. Since the war was arguably most winnable in 1780 after British forces temporarily controlled Georgia and the Carolinas (and Howe was two years gone) the ultimate outcome cannot be blamed solely on Howe. As to Howe's tardy movements, it is clear that he:

- sincerely believed the revolt was instigated and perpetuated by a minority of Americans in 1774-77, and that the majority, if treated leniently with the rights of Englishmen, would return to the Crown once Washington's army inevitably disintegrated.

- was genuinely concerned with the welfare of his soldiers and did not wish to campaign until they were properly provisioned. (Since his 35,000-man army required 37 tons of food and 35 tons of fodder *per day,* and American privateers threatened supply and communications ships, accumulating these supplies took time.)

- was profoundly influenced by the redcoat losses at Bunker Hill (1054 killed and wounded in his 2500-man assault force), and determined never again to sacrifice precious British manpower by attacking well-entrenched American positions with his limited resources. Instead he attempted either to draw Washington into the field (Brandywine & Germantown), or resorted to flanking strategies (Long Island & Westchester County).

- upon learning his troop requests for the 1777 campaign would not be granted by London, and realizing that Washington could not be lured from his trenches (except on his own terms), Howe concluded after Saratoga that the war was not winnable with the resources at his disposal, and refused to put his army at risk.

After a comfortable winter in Mrs. Loring's arms on the Philadelphia social circuit, Sir William then resigned his command the following spring.

[21] Hadaway, William S., editor, *The McDonald Papers*, Part I, New York: Knickerbocker Press for the Westchester County Historical Society, 1927. p.101

[22] Robertson, p. 127.

[23] As quoted from Reverend Edward Teller by Hamilton D. Hurd, *History of Fairfield County, Connecticut*, Philadelphia: J.W. Lewis & Company, 1881. p. 646.

[24] Bedini, p. 204. Rockwell family records attribute Abraham Rockwell's actions to his daughter Lucy, who also volunteered that a severe skirmish took place a few rods from his house.

[25] Scott Family papers as quoted in Bedini, p. 64.

[26] Ibid.

[27] Letter from Mr. John Campbell to Gen. McDougall, as published in *The Pennsylvania Evening Post* of Thursday, May 1, 1777, Vol.III, Num.346, in the collection of the Danbury Historical Society.

IV. The Patriot Militia Strikes!

[1] *Dispatch from Brigadier General Gold Selleck Silliman to Governor John Trumbull, Fairfield, 29 April 1777.* Manuscript copy in the Fairfield Historical Society, believed to be in his own hand. Silliman counted 600 men with himself, Wooster and Arnold at Bethel, noting that an additional 150 militia under Major Beardsley were nearby along with 50 Continentals under Colonel Jedediah Huntington.

[2] *Letter from George Washington to David Wooster dated March 11, 1777.* George Washington Papers at the Library of Congress 1741-1799, Series 3b Varick Transcripts, letter book #2, image # 370.

[3] Buel, p. 167.

[4] Dann, John C., Editor. *The Revolution Remembered, Eyewitness Accounts of the War for Independence*, Chicago: University of Chicago Press, 1980, pp. 77-79.

[5] *Letter from Colonel Jedediah Huntington to Brigadier General Alexander McDougall dated 28 April 1777.*

[6] Teller, Daniel W. *The History of Ridgefield, Conn., From the First Settlement to the Present Time*, (Danbury, Ct.: T. Donovan, 1878), p. 68.

[7] Venus, Richard. "Dick's Dispatches," # 11, August 12, 1982, *The Ridgefield Press.*

[8] Rockwell, George Lounsbury. *A History of Ridgefield, Connecticut*, reprinted from the original edition privately printed by the author, 1927. New York: Harbor Hill Books, 1979. p. 109.

[9] Case, p. 31. James Bailey's History of Danbury referred to this incident thirty-one years earlier so it is likely that Case relied upon this fellow Danburian.

[10] McDevitt, p. 53.

[11] Bedini, p. 66.

[12] Mollo, John, and McGregor, Malcolm. *Uniforms of the American Revolution,* London: Blandford Press, 1975. p. 13.

[13] Bayles, Lois. "Canaan Parish and the American Revolution," New Canaan Historical Society Annual Report, 1976, vol. VII, no. 2, p. 61.

[14] Bailey, James. *History of Danbury,* New York: Burr Printing House, 1896. p. 100.

[15] Lt. General J. Burgoyne's *A State of the Expedition from Canada, 1780,* Second Appendix No. XIV, p. LIV, as quoted in Gerald Howson's *Burgoyne of Saratoga,* New York: Times Books, 1979. p. 237.

[16] Benedict, Henry Marvin. *The Genealogy of the Benedicts in America,* Albany: Joel Munsell, 1870, p. 367. Colonel Cooke was the husband of Sarah Benedict.

V. Decision at the Barricade

[1] Circa 1870 hand-drawn map of the Stebbins Property, located in *Town of Ridgefield Map and Survey Records,* item #443.

[2] Johnston, Henry P., Editor. *The Record of Connecticut Men in the Military and Naval Service During the War of the Revolution 1775-1783,* Hartford: Case Lockwood, Brainard Company, 1889. pp. 492-93.

[3] *Letter from Brigadier Benedict Arnold to Brigadier General Alexander McDougall from Saugatuck, 28 April 1777.* Papers of the Continental Congress, National Archives Microcopy M-247, reel 186, item 169, vol. 3, pp. 197-98.

[4] *Letter dated Fishkill, 3rd May, 1777 from Hugh Hughes to General Horatio Gates* in the possession of the New York Historical Society.

[5] *Revolutionary War Pension Application of Nehemiah Banks of Fairfield, CT.,* National Archives Record Group # 15, Pension # S12974. Washington D.C.

[6] Todd, Charles Burr. *The History of Redding, Connecticut,* New York: Grafton Press, 1906, p. 31.

[7] *Letter dated Ridgefield, March 14, 1777 from Colonel Philip Burr Bradley to General George Washington* in the collection of Washington's papers in the Library of Congress.

[8] Betz, F. Lee. "Ridgefield's Continentals, Men of the 5th Connecticut Regiment," an eleven page monograph in the possession of the Keeler Tavern Preservation Society, dated 16 March 1986.

[9] Hoadley, Charles J. *Public Records of the State of Connecticut 1776-78,* Hartford: Case, Brainard Company, 1894. p. 203. For more about Connecticut military uniforms during the Revolution, see the Lefferts collection in the possession of the New York Historical Society, and the following documents: *Records of the Colony of Connecticut 1775-1776,* vol. XV, 484; *Records of the State of Connecticut 1776-1778,* vol. 1, 396, 476; *Connecticut Gazette,* April 25, 1777.

[10] Keeler Tavern Society Museum Archives, Betts Collection, item # 3271. Letter dated November 29, 1780 from Norwalk Town Selectmen, certifying Dover Davison was the property of Stephen St. John.

[11] Bedini, pp. 89-90.

[12] *Records of the American Revolution,* Connecticut State Library, Hartford, Series I, Vol. VII, p. 227.

[13] Office of the New York State Controller, *New York in the Revolution,* Albany: J. B. Lyon Company, 1904. p. 149.

[14] Van Norden, Theodore Langdon. *South Salem Soldiers and Sailors,* Lancaster, PA: Lancaster Press, 1927. p. 60.

[15] *The McDonald Papers,* Volume IV, page 131. A personal history of the Revolutionary War in Westchester County, New York, comprised of 407 interviews with 207 persons aged 70-96 between 1844 and 1850. The papers are in the possession of the Westchester County Historical Society.

[16] McDonald, Vol. IV, p. 111.

[17] Hadaway, *The McDonald Papers,* pp. 119-120.

[18] Rockwell, p. 113.

[19] Bedini, p. 80.

[20] Venus, Richard. "Dick's Dispatches #10," *The Ridgefield Press,* 5 August 1982.

[21] Nelson, Paul David. *William Tryon and the Course of Empire,* Chapel Hill: University of North Carolina Press, 1990. pp. 9 & 10.

[22] *Pennsylvania Gazette,* May 14, 1777; *Pennsylvania Evening Post,* May 22, 1777; *South Carolina Gazette,* July 23, 1777.

[23] Bland, Humphrey. *An Abstract of Military Discipline,* Boston: Edward Harvey, 1747. Chapter Four.

[24] Rockwell, p. 124.

[25] Bedini, p. 69.

[26] Lathrop, Cornelia Penfield. *Black Rock, Seaport of Old Fairfield, CT 1644-1870, Including the Wheeler Journal,* New Haven: The Tuttle, Morehouse and Taylor Company, 1930. p. 28.

[27] *Revolutionary War Pension Applications,* National Archives Record Group 15 of the Records of the Veterans Administration.

[28] McDonald, Vol. IV, p. 109.

[29] Lathrop, p. 28.

[30] Wilcoxson, p. 73.

[31] Orcutt, Reverend Samuel. *History of Stratford and Bridgeport, Conn. 1639-1886,* New Haven: The Tuttle, Morehouse and Taylor Company, 1886. p. 376.

[32] Orcutt, p. 377.

[33] *Letter from John Brooks of Stratford to Royal H. Hinman in 1841,* as quoted by Bedini, p. 71.

[34] McDonald, Vol. IV, p. 130.

[35] *The Connecticut Journal,* Wednesday, April 30, 1777, #498, New Haven: Printed by Thomas and Samuel Green.

[36] Lossing, Benson J. *Pictorial Fieldbook of the Revolution,* New York: Harper Brothers, 1851. p. 409.

[37] Case, p. 34.

[38] Huntington, Revered E. B. *History of Stamford,* Stamford, CT: William W. Gillespie & Company, 1868. p. 245.

[39] Grumman, William. *The Revolutionary Soldiers of Redding,* Hartford: Hartford Press, 1904. p.71.

[40] The McDonald Papers, vol. IV, p. 134.

[41] Letter from Captain G. Hutchinson to Earl Percy from aboard the packet Mercury on Long Island Sound, 30 April 1777, *London Gazette,* 9 June 1777, reprinted in *Lloyd's Evening Post,* 40, no. 113 (6-9 June 1777): 549.

[42] Johnston, p. 493

[43] The formal British returns for the Danbury expedition were published in the *London Gazette* on June 5, 1777 in the form of an extract from a *Letter from the Hon. General Sir William Howe to Lord Geo. Germain, dated New-York, April 24, 1777, received by the* Mercury, *Packet.*

VI. Redcoats Take Ridgefield

[1] Bedini, p. 83. According to an 1841 letter from John Brooks of Stratford to Royal H. Hinman, "Colonel John Benjamin was shot with three buck shot lodged in his neck, which he survived."

[2] Robertson, p. 128.

[3] Welsh, Glenna M. *The Proprietors of Ridgefield,* Ridgefield, CT: Caudatowa Press, 1976. p. 133.

[4] Goodrich, Samuel Griswold. *Recollections of a Lifetime: or Men and Things I Have Seen,* New York: Miller, Orton, and Mulligan, 1856. p. 21.

[5] Bedini, p. 90.

[6] Case, pp. 35-36

[7] Robertson, p. 128.

[8] ibid.

[9] Teller, Daniel. *The History of Ridgefield,* Danbury: T. Donovan, 1878. p. 71.

[10] The red petticoat story is part of Ridgefield lore that has been repeated by Goodrich, Teller, Rockwell, and Bedini. Whether true or not, it is quite probable given the location of Captain David Olmstead's house only a few rods away from the two Northrop dwellings that *were* burned. This particular version is taken from *Heritage '76 Ridgefield: A Place in Time,* The Bicentennial Commission, Ridgefield: 1976. p. 34. A full-length fictionalized account of what might have happened continues to hold young girls spellbound in Joan E. Palmer's *The Red Petticoat,* New York: Lothrup, Lee & Shepard Company, 1964

[11] Robertson, p. 128.

[12] McDonald, Volume IV, p. 134.

[13] McDonald, Volume II, p. 173

[14] Johnston, p. 493.

VII. Aftermath

[1] *Letter from George Washington to Continental Congress dated May 24, 1777.* George Washington Papers at the Library of Congress 1741-1799, Series 3b Varick Transcripts, letter book # 2, image #276.

[2] Letter from Colonel Hugh Hughes to General Horatio Gates, 3 May 1777, *Gates Papers,* The New York Historical Society.

[3] *Comprehensive Report of the Committee appointed by the General Assembly to investigate Sufferer Claims in Ridgefield dated 5 December 1777.* (Revolutionary War Manuscript Collection of the Connecticut State Archives, Hartford, Ct.) reproduced by Bedini, p. 129. See Appendix C for the full text.

[4] *Journals of the Continental Congress 1774-1789,* Wednesday, April 30, 1777, Volume VII, p. 315.

[5] Letter from John Adams to Nathaniel Greene, Philadelphia, May 9, 1777. *Letters of Delegates to Congress, 1774-1789,* Edited by Paul H. Smith et al. Washington, D.C. Volume 7, p. 49.

[6] Knight, Henry. *Orderly Book of British Headquarters, Feb. 14, 1777-June 2, 1777 kept by Capt. Henry Knight, Aide-de-camp to Lord Howe,* New York Historical Society, May 2, 9, & 10.   Howe's commendation of May 2 also appeared in the orderly books of other regiments as follows: "The Commander-in-chief Returns his thanks to Major Gen^L Tryon, to the Gen^L Officers and to all the other officers under his command, on the Last Expedition the Regularity of the men reflects Credit upon the Discipline of the Army and does them great honor."   For a detailed account of Tryon's efforts to gain recognition and reward for his role in the Danbury raid, see Paul David Nelson's *William Tryon and the Course of Empire* (Chapel Hill: University of North Carolina Press, 1990), pp. 152-159.

[7] Marshall, Douglas and Peckham, Howard. *Campaigns of the American Revolution,* Ann Arbor: University of Michigan Press, 1976. p. 37.

[8] *Letter from Lord, Sir William Howe to Lord George Germain, dated Boston, 1775.* Force, Peter, *American Archives,* Fourth Series [March 7, 1774, to July 4, 1776], Volume 5, pp. 926-27.

[9] Fred Anderson, *Crucible of War: The Seven Years War and the Fate of Empire in British North America. 1754-1766,* (New York: Vintage Books, 2001), p. 519.

[10] *Letter from Lord, Sir William, Howe to Benjamin Franklin,* dated June 20, 1776, as quoted by H. W. Brands, *The First American: The Life and Times of Benjamin Franklin,* New York: Doubleday, 2000. p. 515.

[11] Commodore Sir George Collier and Major-General William Tryon, Broadside of an *Address to the Inhabitants of Connecticut,* July 4, 1779. George Washington papers at the Library of Congress, 1741-1799: Series 4. General Correspondence 1697-1799, Image # 1034 & 1035,

[12] Letter from John Burgoyne to George Germain, August 12, 1777, *The Remembrancer (1777).* Appendix: p. xxv.

[13] Letter from Lewis Morris Jr., to his father, General Lewis Morris, September 6, 1776. New York Historical Society, Collection VIII (1875), p. 442.

[14] Letter from Washington to Wharton, October 17, 1777 as quoted by Beveridge, Albert J. *The Life of John Marshall,* Washington, D.C.: Beard Books, 1916. Vol. I, p. 85.

[15] Burr, William Hanford. "The Invasion of Connecticut by the British," *Connecticut Magazine,* January 1906, pp. 139-152.

[16] *Ridgefield Town Meeting Records,* 1746-1797, p. 63.

[17] Goodrich, Samuel G. *Recollections of a Lifetime, or Men and Things I have Seen; In a Series of Familiar Letters to a Friend, Historical, Biographical,*

Anecdotal, and Descriptive, 2 vols. New York and Auburn: Miller, Orton & Mulligan, 1857. p. 115.

VIII. Epilogue

[1] Danenberg, Elise N. *The Romance of Norwalk*, New York: States History Company, 1929. p. 149.
[2] Sheftail, John McKay. *The Dimons of Fairfield, Connecticut, A Family History,* Roswell, Georgia: W. H. Wolfe Associates, 1983. p. 445.

About the Author

Historic house aficionado and long time student of the American Revolution, Keith Marshall Jones is President of the Ridgefield Historical Society, chairman of the Battle of Ridgefield 225th Reenactment Committee, and author of *The Farms of Farmingville*. Keith and his family inhabit an early Federal farmhouse erected by Revolutionary War pensioner Nehemiah Banks some twelve years after hostilities ceased.

Order Form

Customer Order No._____

Date _____

Connecticut Colonel
Publishing Company

304 Farmingville Road
Ridgefield, Connecticut, 06877
ct.colonel@snet.net

Please ship _____copies of

Farmers Against the Crown

By Keith Marshall Jones III

Soft Cover Price: $18.95 + Postage

*Library Price: $3/copy discount

Buyers Signature_____

Ship to:

     NAME_____

     STREET_____

     CITY_____STATE_____ZIP_____

More about Connecticut Farmers

The Farms of Farmingville, by Keith Marshall Jones III, is the story of twenty-three farmhouses in one eighteenth-century Connecticut school district, and the generations of real people who gave them life. With **more than 100 photos and illustrations**, Jones's book explains:

- ❖ How a colonial farmhouse was built
- ❖ What the everyday life of a local farm family was like
- ❖ How local domestic architecture evolved from 1720 to 1920
- ❖ The individual history of 23 surviving dwellings and 24 lost farms
- ❖ How the local school, church, mills, physician, bank, and even the cemetery functioned
- ❖ How stone "farmer's" walls were built
- ❖ Why area farmers were ultimately doomed by economics

"A delightful book" writes Connecticut State Historian, Christopher Collier, and a *"marvelous guide to the environs and houses so nicely presented." "Much more interesting than just another 'What Style Is It?' discussion"* observes Christopher Wigren, Assistant Director of the Connecticut Trust for Historic Preservation. Mail order inquiries about *The Farms of Farmingville* may be directed to the author at the following address:

Connecticut Colonel Publishing Company
304 Farmingville Road
Ridgefield, CT 06877